HOW TO WIN AT
CHESS

HOW TO WIN AT
CHESS

**THE ULTIMATE GUIDE FOR
BEGINNERS AND BEYOND**

LEVY ROZMAN

TEN SPEED PRESS
California | New York

To my fans, who have supported me throughout my journey.

To my family, who introduced me to this beautiful game.

And to Lucy, who changed my life.

CONTENTS

INTRODUCTION

Hello and welcome! My name is Levy. I'm an International Master, a former semi-professional player, and now I primarily teach chess online. Before we dive into the specifics of how to win at chess, I'd like to give you some background about myself, this book, and the basics of this incredible game.

Chess is a fascinating game, but our learning material can be quite intimidating. Throughout my years as a chess instructor, countless people have asked me, "What is a good first chess book to buy?" The truth is, nobody has a definitive answer! In my experience, beginner and intermediate chess books vary greatly in length and depth, and usually require having a physical chessboard on hand to follow along with the instructions. The search for a comprehensive, modern guide to chess was my inspiration for the book you currently hold in your hands. My goal was to write a refreshing, revitalized take on this timeless and beautifully complicated game.

I've spent nearly my entire adult life teaching chess to others. Whether it was in kindergarten classes or corporate offices, I always searched for the most effective means of demystifying the 64 squares to my students. When the world shut down in the early days of the COVID-19 pandemic in 2020, I began teaching my students on Zoom, but forcing six-year-old kids to sit through private chess lessons online was both fruitless and mildly depressing, so I turned my focus to YouTube. In the years since then, I have made a video about chess nearly every day of my life.

Some of you might have found me on YouTube a few years back, and my videos became your reprieve during hard times. Others may have watched me back in 2018, as a disheveled mess livestreaming at 4 a.m. on Twitch. And the rest of you may not have a clue about my online endeavors but are simply curious about learning chess—just know that I deeply appreciate all of you. I love making the game fun and accessible to everyone, which I hope will become clear to you in the chapters ahead. Over the next several pages, you will learn the fundamental rules of the game, to which you can refer back at any point in your learning and play as a refresher. Then the real lessons begin. Enjoy!

The Basics of Chess

Chess is nearly 1,500 years old, and its origins can be traced back to sixth-century India. The game has gone through some changes since then but today, the board looks like this:

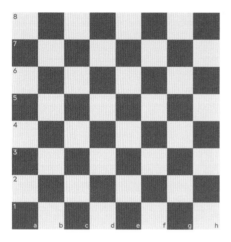

⬆ A chessboard has 64 squares, laid out in a grid of 8 x 8. The squares alternate between light and dark. The bottom right-hand corner should be a light square for both players, whether you're playing with an actual board or online.

The board has coordinates, too. An online board will likely have the coordinates showing on the board (like the board above)—but most real boards don't. Think of the coordinates as a simple road map. The vertical lines of a chessboard—called **files**—are named a through h going from left to right. The horizontal rows—called **ranks**—are numbered from 1 through 8, going from bottom to top. This means that any square on the chessboard can be identified by combining the file letter with the rank number:

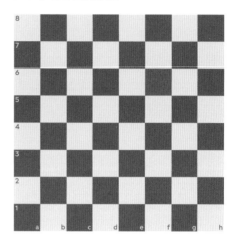

⬆ The highlighted square here, for example, is on the f file and the 6th rank. This square is therefore f6. (The letter always comes first.)

Now let's add the pieces. This is the starting position for a game of chess:

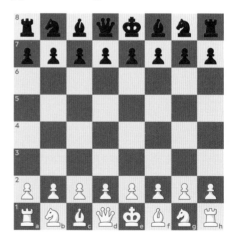

White begins on the 1st and 2nd ranks, while Black begins on the 7th and 8th ranks. Each side has 16 pieces, meaning a total of 32 pieces on the board. This is how the pieces should always be configured. We'll introduce each piece next but for now, it's important to know how the pieces should be set up. Both players have a row of pawns with their major pieces behind them. Everything is symmetrical, including the kings and queens, which should be set up opposite one another—the queens should begin on the d file and the kings on the e file.

In chess, players take turns to move the pieces. White always moves first. We'll get into how to begin the game and how to win a game of chess in the coming chapters, but before that we should introduce the pieces.

This is the **queen**. The queen is worth 9 points, making it the most valuable piece (excluding the king, which we'll come to next). It's worth noting that the "points" value of each piece is hypothetical and is only meant to express their value relative to other pieces. Each player only gets one queen. The queen can move up, down, left, right, and diagonally—and can move as many squares as it wants, providing those squares are not obstructed. The queen cannot move through or hop over other pieces, including those of the same color. On an empty chessboard, the queen could move to any of the squares along these ranks, files, or diagonals. The queen is your most powerful piece; no other piece can move in so many different directions and go as far as it wants. ✐

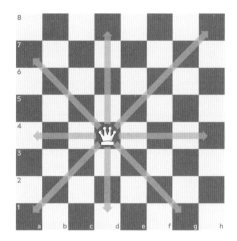

The **rook** is your second most valuable piece (again excluding the king), worth 5 points. You start the game with two rooks. The rook is able to move up, down, left, and right in any direction, and as many squares as it wants, providing those squares aren't obstructed by other pieces. ⬇

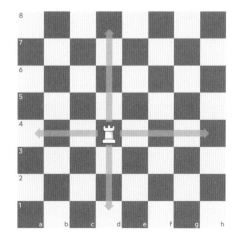

The **bishop** is worth three points. Each player starts with two bishops, one on a light square and the other on a dark square. A bishop can move as many squares as it wants (again providing those squares aren't obstructed by other pieces), but only move diagonally. That means that your light-squared bishop will always live on the light squares of the board and vice versa for your dark-squared bishop. ↓

A **knight** is also worth 3 points and each player starts with two knights. The knight moves in the most unique way of all the pieces and is also unique in that it's the only piece on the board that can hop over other pieces—whether its own pieces or the opponent's. The knight moves in an L-shape, so up, down, or across two squares and then one square to

the side. This diagram shows all the squares a knight in the center of an empty board can jump to. ↓

Since the knight can hop over pieces, it is the only piece on the back rank that can immediately jump into play from the start of the game. The other pieces need a clear path, which comes from moving pawns. ↓

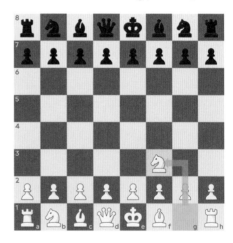

A **pawn** is worth 1 point and each player begins with eight pawns. There are five rules associated with pawns that you need to know.

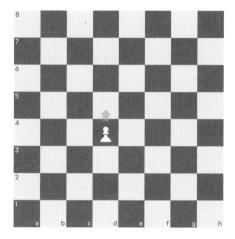

⬆ Pawns can move one square forward at a time. However, on their first move—and only then—each pawn has the option to move two squares forward rather than one.

✎ In the Openings chapters of this book (pages 24–49), we'll explore the different situations in which a pawn might choose to move one square or two; for now, it's just important to know that each player has the option of pushing each of their eight pawns either one or two squares forward on that pawn's first move. After that, pawns can only move one square forward.

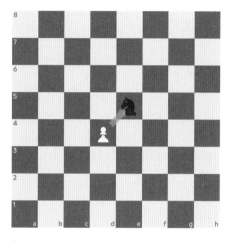

⬆ But when a pawn **captures**—which is when one piece moves onto a square occupied by an enemy piece, thus removing that enemy piece from the game—the pawn moves diagonally. The pawn cannot move diagonally into an empty square; likewise the pawn cannot capture another piece vertically. It can only move into an empty square straight up and can only capture diagonally. Still with me?

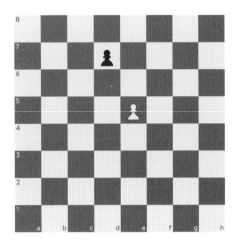

⬆ Another very interesting rule with pawns is that when they reach the far side of the board (for White that would be the 8th rank, for Black the 1st rank), they **promote**. This means the pawn becomes either a knight, bishop, rook, or queen—the player chooses. In most cases, you'd choose to promote to a queen because it's the most powerful piece, but there are rare situations where you might promote to another piece instead. In theory, you could march all eight pawns up the board, promote them to queens, and have nine queens.

⬆ And the bonus rule of pawns is something called **en passant**, which is the weirdest rule in chess. If you look at the above position, White's pawn is beyond the halfway point of the board and Black's pawn on d7 is in its starting position. This means that the player with the Black pieces may choose to move their pawn forward two squares, like this. ⬇

Having moved forward two squares, the Black pawn now stands adjacent to the White pawn (which is on e5). In this situation, only for the turn immediately after Black made that move, White has the option to capture the Black pawn, even though the Black pawn was standing adjacent to the White pawn instead of standing diagonally from it. ⬇

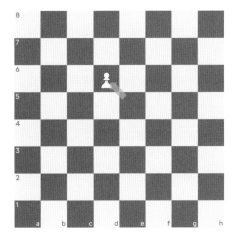

This is the only capture in chess where the capturing piece ends up on a different square to the piece that was captured. Essentially, you are capturing the opposing pawn on the square it would have moved to if it had only moved one square on its first move rather than two.

As I said, this is the weirdest move in chess and can take a while to get your head around. It only occurs when a pawn jumps forward two squares on its first move and lands adjacent to an opposing pawn. The player then has the choice whether or not to take *en passant* (it isn't obligatory, just like any capture). But if you don't take *en passant* in the turn immediately after the opposing pawn moves up two squares and lands next to your pawn, you miss the chance to capture this way, since you can't execute *en passant* later on. Only pawns can *en passant*, and it only applies to capturing other pawns.

Finally, we need to look at the **king**. Like the queen, each player has only one king. The king is unique in that it can never be captured. It therefore has no point value, unlike the other pieces. It's essentially worth either zero or infinity depending on your point of view. Your king is your most important piece. A game of chess is won or lost when your king is checkmated, which is when a piece is threatening to capture it and your king has nowhere safe to go. We will look at checkmates in more detail in the coming chapters. A king can only ever move one square, though it can move in any direction. ⬇

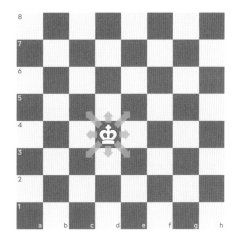

A king cannot move itself into danger, though—it cannot move into a square that would allow it to be captured by an enemy piece. This would be an illegal move. Any other piece can move into danger and simply be captured by an opposing piece. No chess website will allow you to move your king into danger—it's not that you would lose, it just isn't allowed within the rules of chess.

↑ There's also a bonus rule related to kings, which is known as **castling**. On the board here, we see the starting squares for White's king and rooks. Castling is the ability to get your king to a safer position by sliding it two squares over toward one of the rooks, with the rook jumping over to the other side of the king. There are a couple of criteria that have to be met for castling to be allowed.

First, you cannot have already moved your king or the rook that you want to castle toward. Next, you also cannot castle through danger—so if an enemy piece would be able to capture your king on one of the squares

your king is passing through, castling won't be allowed. There also can't be any of your own pieces between the king and the rook. ↓

You can either castle "short" (i.e., kingside), which leaves your king and rook in the above position. Or you can castle "long" (i.e., queenside), which looks like this. ↓

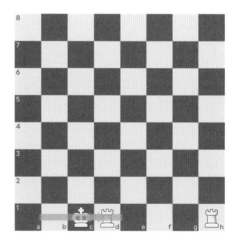

We'll look at when to castle in more depth in later chapters, but in essence, the idea is to move your king to a safer spot in the corner while also bringing your rook into the middle, where it's more effective. This is the only move in chess where you can move two pieces at the same time.

I know that's a lot of pieces and a lot of rules. If you're a beginner and already frustrated or confused, don't be. Everybody goes through this process. I promise it only gets better from here and you'll quickly pick up how all the pieces move and how and when these rules and special moves apply.

↑ The final thing to note about kings is when one is attacked, that is a **check**. In this example, the Black bishop "sees" the White king and is threatening to capture it. In chess, if you are in check then you must make a move to get out of check. When in check, it's illegal

to make any move that doesn't get your king out of check. So, a check must be addressed— later, we'll look in more detail about ways to get out of check.

The other two situations involving a king are **checkmate** and **stalemate**—both of which we'll look at more in the chapters to come. Checkmate is attacking the king in a way where it cannot escape, which means the checkmating player wins the game. Stalemate is a situation where the king is not in check but the player has no legal moves, that is, the king would have to *move into* check, which is illegal, and the player is unable to move any other pieces. Therefore, stalemate means a draw. I know, I know—this is a lot of stuff. But I promise it's easier than golf or baseball. More fun, too!

So, that's an introduction to the pieces and the rules. I don't expect you to remember everything, and don't worry—we're going to cover everything in more detail, beginning with checkmates and how to literally win a game of chess.

Chess Notation

Chess notation describes how moves in a game of chess are recorded and described. You don't need to know this to play chess but it's something to be aware of as you advance your understanding of the game. We talked about how every square has a coordinate—these form one part of the notation for every move. The other part is the piece moving to the square. The below table outlines how each piece is described in chess notation:

Pawn	With pawns, only the square being moved to is described, e.g., "e6" means a pawn has moved to the e6 square. If a pawn captures onto a square, you include where it came from: "exd5."
Bishop	B
Knight	N
Rook	R
Queen	Q
King	K

In chess notation, a pawn move is the only piece that doesn't reference the piece in question. You'll notice a knight uses "N," which is to avoid getting confused with the "K" for king.

Let's look at an example so you can see how chess notation works in practice:

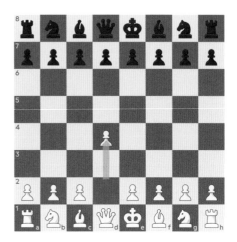

⬆ White has pushed their d pawn two squares to d4. In chess notation, this would be "1. d4." The "1" indicates it's the first move and "d4," without a piece reference, tells us it's a pawn move.

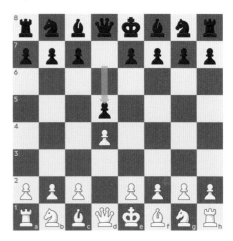

⬆ When Black responds by pushing their own d pawn two squares, the notation for the first move is completed as "1. d4 d5."

♙ Let's say White uses their second move to bring out their bishop and Black moves their knight to c6. The notation for move 2 would be "2. Bf4 Nc6." Here "B" describes the bishop and "N" describes Black's knight.

The notation then continues in the same way for every move of the game. Typical of chess, there are a few nuances you also need to be aware of. When one piece captures another, we add an "x" between the piece and the square coordinate. For example, if White's queen captures a Black piece on the d2 square, we write "Qxd2."

If a move is a check on the opposing king, we add a "+" symbol at the end of the notation. For example, if our rook moves to h8 and checks the opposing king, the notation would be "Rh8+." Similarly, there's an additional symbol if it's checkmate. Imagine the same move is instead checkmate—this would be recorded as "Rh8#."

When a pawn promotes, we add an "=" symbol between the move and the piece that the pawn has promoted to. For instance, imagine we have a pawn on the g7 square. When we move the pawn to g8, we can promote it to any of a bishop, knight, rook, or queen. If we choose a queen (which is the most common choice, given that a queen is the best piece), we'd write "g8=Q." Alternatively, it would be "g8=B" for a bishop, "g8=N" for a knight, or "g8=R" for a rook.

Castling is notated as O-O when a player castles short/kingside and O-O-O when a player castles long/queenside.

There's one final detail about chess notation I need to cover before moving on. Look at the following position:

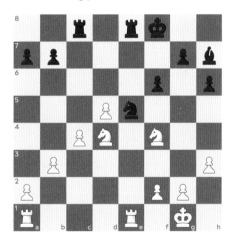

♙ In this position, White wants to move their knight on f4 to the e6 square. However, both of White's knights could move to this square, so the notation "Ne6" doesn't work, since the White knight on d4 could also move to e6. In this case, we'd instead write "Nfe6,"

with the additional "f" indicating it's the knight on the f file (rather than the knight on the d file) making this move. This comes up particularly with knights and rooks, as pairs of knights or rooks can sometimes land on the same square. Extra detail is therefore required to indicate which piece is making the move. Knights or rooks could also be on the same file and still "see" the same square—in those instances, you'd use the rank number to indicate which piece is moving (i.e., "N2d3," where the "2" after "N" shows it's the knight on the second rank making the move).

Scoring

A game of chess can be won, lost, or drawn. We'll explore how the different results are reached in chess in the coming chapters. In tournament chess, a win typically earns the player 1 point while a draw means each player gets ½ a point. Unsurprisingly, you get 0 for a loss. As of 2022, some tournaments have been exploring 3 points for a win and 1 point each for a draw to make a win more rewarding. At the top level, grandmasters can often settle for draws in a way you don't see with many other sports, which can be frustrating for fans.

Winning, drawing, or losing also affects your rating. A chess rating is called Elo, named after its creator, Hungarian-American physics professor Arpad Elo, that quantifies your skill level relative to other players. You get an Elo when playing in sanctioned, over-the-board tournaments as well as playing on any major chess website (though playing casually online

means your Elo isn't official). The lowest possible Elo, both online and over the board, is 100. The highest ever over-the-board Elo was achieved by Magnus Carlsen in 2014, with a rating of 2882. Online rating technically has no ceiling but 3300–3400 seems to be the highest.

There are variances between Elo depending on which website you play on, as well as in which country you play for sanctioned over-the-board tournaments. FIDE, the International Chess Federation, is considered the most official Elo throughout the world for over-the-board chess.

Practicing Chess

A lot of tips, tricks, and useful ideas will be introduced in this book, but you will never improve at chess without lots of practice. This goes for openings, tactics, checkmates, and everything in between. But how do you actually practice chess? The chess learning ecosystem has a few components you should get familiar with.

Playing Games

Playing chess games from start to finish, either online or offline, is the most important way to practice. Most games have a timer per player that ticks down whenever a certain side is to move. In blitz chess, for example, each players gets three minutes for the entire game. In classical chess, each side may get three hours. Whatever the time control, whatever the format, playing lots of games is the best way to build on what you've learned.

Chess Engines

A computer program can analyze chess positions, giving an evaluation and recommending best moves for both sides. Modern chess engines such as Stockfish have Elo strengths of approximately 3700, compared to the highest human Elo of all time at 2882.

Game Analysis

Once you complete a live game, it is best to review it either with a stronger chess player or a chess engine. When you play online, your moves are recorded and saved to your account; when you play in person, you usually have to notate your moves by hand at tournaments. Reviewing your games will help you play your openings correctly and identify your strengths and weaknesses as a player. If you analyze with a chess engine, you are responsible for figuring out why the computer suggests certain improvements. A human, however, can not only spot your mistakes, but can also explain them to you to prevent future recurrences.

Chess Bots

Most chess websites have a section where you can play live games against "weaker" chess engines that simulate lower-Elo opponents. Some players enjoy practicing against bots because of the anxiety that comes with playing live chess games against other humans. Personally, I am not a fan of playing against bots, because they do not correctly emulate human chess behavior and are programmed to self-destruct, essentially granting you victory.

Puzzles

Chess puzzles are specific positions, usually with one solution, that are designed to train your awareness of a certain concept. The most elementary type of puzzle is "Checkmate In 1," where you must make a move that delivers checkmate, winning the game immediately. The stronger you get at chess, the longer chess puzzles become—sometimes you must visualize more than 5 moves ahead for both yourself and the opponent.

Chess puzzles come in print and digital form. For years, chess workbooks existed that featured thousands of training positions on checkmates, tactics, and strategic play. In the modern era, every major chess website has hundreds of thousands of puzzles on many different concepts.

Additional Learning Material

To help with practicing different concepts and deepening your understanding, there are exclusive QR codes at the end of each chapter. Simply scan the QR codes with your device and you'll be taken to a set of puzzles or lessons that I have created for you related to the topics covered in each chapter. These might be checkmating puzzles, detailed explanations of openings or gambits, or practical examples of certain endgame scenarios.

PART ONE   0-800 ELO

Welcome to Part One!
In this portion of the book, you will learn the following:

1. **How chess games are actually won, lost, and drawn**

2. **The best way to start a chess game with White and Black**

3. **Basic checkmates in the endgame**

4. **Checkmating combinations in the middlegame**

5. **How chess pieces interact: attack, defense, and various tactics**

6. **Various fundamental chess strategies: weaknesses, space, and more**

In chess—especially online—the term *Elo* quantifies the skill level of a player. I recommend Part One to players in the 0–800 Elo range, as well as to more advanced players who need to review basic concepts now and then. In noncompetitive terms, Part One is for players ranging from total newcomers to relatively experienced beginners.

You may find that you already know some of what's discussed in the coming chapters, but I am hopeful that most of the text will be enlightening and fun to read. Please enjoy!

CHAPTER ONE
HOW TO (LITERALLY) WIN AT CHESS

I decided the best way to start a book called *How to Win at Chess* would be with a chapter explaining exactly what it actually means—and how it is possible—to literally win a chess game. As you know by now, this is the starting position for any game of chess: ⬇

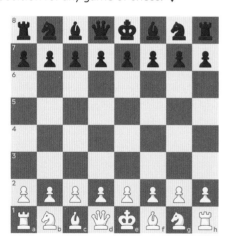

Each side has sixteen pieces. Many of them move in different ways and have different rules for how they can move. The bottom-left square should be a dark square, and all the pieces should be arranged in perfect symmetry. Now the two sides are ready to go to battle.

Perhaps you *didn't* know that learning to play chess should start with as few pieces as possible. If we start with all thirty-two pieces on the board, things might get confusing pretty quickly because beginning with too much information can be overwhelming. A better way to begin is to look at what it means to win a game of chess and how you can do it. After all, that's what the book is called and what we ultimately care about, right?

Checkmate

Most games of chess are won by **checkmate**. Checkmate is when you create an attack—a threat to capture—the enemy king, and there is no way for your opponent to get out of that situation. In chess, the king is the only piece that can never be captured. Attacking the enemy king in a way where the king cannot escape is checkmate and the end of the game. The following diagram is the simplest example of a checkmate:

Here is an example of a checkmate with four pieces on the board: ⬇

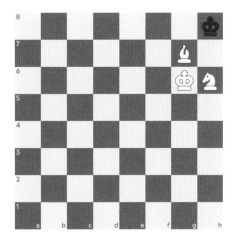

⬆ In the position we see here, Black's king is being attacked by the White queen. Because a king can only move one square at a time, there is nowhere the Black king can move where it wouldn't be captured by the White queen on White's next move. The Black king also cannot capture the White queen because the White king defends it (meaning that the Black king cannot capture the White queen, because otherwise the White king would be in a position to capture the Black king on the next move, which can never happen in chess).

We will learn more about how each piece moves, attacks, and defends later on, but for now I really want to stress that the minimum number of pieces you need on the board to create a checkmate is three. Think about that. That is a much simpler point to begin learning the game than the starting position, where we have thirty-two pieces on the board!

White's bishop attacks the Black king, White's king defends its own bishop, and all three White pieces together—bishop, king, and knight take away all available escape squares for the Black king.

Now that I've shown you a couple of checkmate examples with a minimum number of pieces on the board, let's look at an example with a fully populated board. The principles here are exactly the same—the king is being attacked and has no safe square to escape.

▲ Anywhere that Black's king moves, it would be captured by a White piece on the next move. That means checkmate and the end of the game. Clearly Black did something catastrophically incorrect here. The king is the most important piece and should not be in the center of battle between the opposing sets of pieces. (This book will help you avoid getting yourself into situations like this!) The point here is that checkmate can occur anywhere on the board, and with all the pieces on the board or as few as three (as seen in the example on the previous page).

Checkmate can also happen at the very beginning of a game. One of the most famous checkmating patterns is called the Scholar's Mate.

▲ Here White has checkmated Black in just four moves. White's queen attacks Black's king. Black's king has no safe squares to escape to and cannot capture the White queen because it's defended by White's bishop. According to online chess databases (websites like Chess.com, Lichess, and Chessbase) this position has been reached nearly 1 million times—so it can and does happen! It's mind-blowing that so many people fall for this very common trap. The good news, however, is that you will never fall for this trick now that you own this book. (Results may vary.)

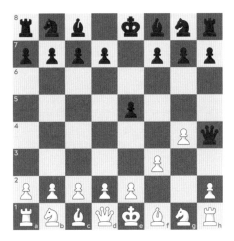

Resignation

The second most common way to win a game of chess is when your opponent resigns. Resignation means surrendering the game, whether because of overwhelming material loss, because you are about to be checkmated and there is no way to avoid it, or because you're playing online and your food delivery arrives before you can finish the game. When playing online, this means clicking the "resign" button. In person, it means letting your opponent know you're resigning and offering a handshake.

In the 2014 World Chess Championship between challenger and former world chess champion Viswanathan Anand and defending world champion Magnus Carlsen, Anand surrendered the eleventh game of the twelve-game match (and therefore the entire match itself) in the following position:

⬆ But the Scholar's Mate is not even the fastest way to lose a game. There's something called the Fool's Mate, where a person can lose the game in just *two* moves, as shown in the diagram.

Here the Black queen on h4 attacks the White king and White's king has no safe square to escape, nor can any of White's other pieces block the check or capture Black's queen. It's therefore a very quick and embarrassing checkmate!

We'll learn some more typical checkmates, including how to build checkmating attacks—and how to identify and defend against your opponent's checkmate threats—later in the book. For now, the most important thing to know is that checkmating your opponent is the most common way to win a game of chess. But it isn't the only way.

 FUN FACT

According to Chess.com's Insights Feature, your humble author has won 55 percent of his games by resignation. The rest were won by time (24 percent), checkmate (20 percent), and abandonment (1 percent).

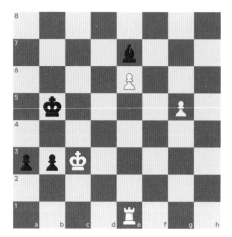

⬆ Carlsen, playing White, would have soon won both of Black's remaining pawns and then pushed one of his own until it became a queen. Then he would have checkmated Anand. Not wanting to spend hours in a terrible position, Anand threw in the towel and resigned.

At the elite level, chess is one of the rare sports where you are supposed to surrender before the opponent checkmates you when checkmate is inevitable—it is considered a sign of disrespect otherwise. This idea of resigning out of respect does not apply to anybody below master level, though. Even if you are losing, whether because you have lost most of your pieces, because of your opponent's threats, or because of the clock—never resign! Make your opponent checkmate you or win on time. While there is time on the clock and pieces on the board, there is the chance your opponent will mess it up by blundering pieces or getting themselves checkmated.

Timing Out

Your opponent running out of time is the next most common way to win a game of chess. Whether you are playing online or over the board, in competitive matches, chess is often played with a timer. Online games can range from one minute to play the entire game (called bullet chess) to as much as fourteen days per move (historically this has been called correspondence chess). Over-the-board chess also has a variety of time controls, with games usually taking 3–6 hours. The most common time control is 90 minutes per player with each player also getting 30 seconds added to their clock whenever they make a move.

Here is an example position from one of my own online games:

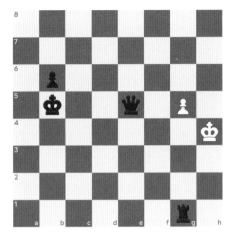

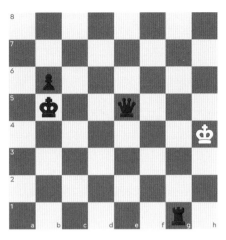

♟ Black has an overwhelming lead here—Black is up a queen and a rook, which is a decisive advantage. If it were Black's turn then they could checkmate White in one move (actually there are two checkmates on the board for Black—try to find them).*

However, if Black's clock hits zero here then White wins the game, despite Black's massive advantage. The clock is part of the game and players must manage their time. For now, don't worry about the clock. You can play chess with friends or against a chess computer without a time control. But bear the clock in mind when you begin playing online or live chess, as it's never fun to lose a game because of time.

There is an extra consideration here before we move on to the next section. Here is an almost identical position to the above, except White doesn't have the pawn on g5:

♟ There is a bonus chess rule called **insufficient checkmating material.** In this position, if Black runs out of time, then the game ends in a draw, rather than a win for White. That's because White doesn't have enough pieces to ever deliver checkmate. White only has a king and you need at least one other piece to checkmate—as we saw earlier in the chapter on page 17, you need at least two pieces to checkmate the opposing king—you could never checkmate the enemy king with only your own king. Don't worry about this rule just yet. These obscure rules can sometimes scare people away from chess or dampen their enthusiasm, but don't let them deter you. (I have to mention this rule here; otherwise somebody will give this book a one-star review because their game ended in a draw when they were expecting a win!)

---

* Queen to h8 is checkmate for Black, and so is queen to h2. In both cases, the White king has nowhere to run!

Abandonment

The fourth, final, and funniest way to win a game of chess is abandonment. Abandonment is when a player simply stops playing rather than resigning or allowing themselves to be checkmated. This is particularly common in online chess, but it happens in over-the-board games, too, as shown in the below example. ⬇

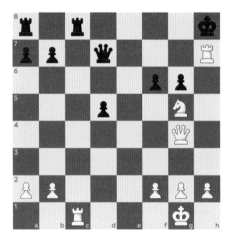

The year is 1895. We are in Hastings, England. Wilhelm Steinitz, the first-ever world chess champion, has the White pieces in this position, playing against Curt von Bardeleben, who has the Black pieces. Von Bardeleben was so disgusted with the position he found himself in—with the brilliance of Steinitz's combinations and with certain defeat looming—that he got up from the board and literally left the building.

Steinitz had to wait for von Bardeleben's clock to hit zero before he officially won the game. Once it had, a peacocking Steinitz—in a display of absolute dominance—demonstrated to the audience that he had foreseen a forced checkmate in nine moves, to which the crowd responded with roaring applause. Maybe von Bardeleben had foreseen the same thing, and that's why he stormed off. To see the full game, use the QR code on the following page.

Summary

Chapter One is based, quite literally, on the title of this book. This was a deliberate decision, so that you could understand how to actually finish a chess game with a win. Here is a quick summary of all the different ways a chess game can be won (or lost!).

1. Checkmate is an attack on a king that cannot be stopped. The king cannot move to escape, no pieces can block the attack, and nothing can capture the attacker. The king in danger would be captured on the next move.

2. Resignation is essentially surrendering. One might resign when down a significant number of pieces—say a queen, a rook, a knight, or any combination of the three.

3. Timing out occurs when you play with a clock and your allotted time hits zero before the game is over. Remember, your clock only runs on your move, so if you are playing with a clock you must ration your remaining minutes responsibly. The bonus to this rule is called "insufficient checkmating material"—if, say, your time runs out but your opponent only has a king remaining, they do not have a necessary amount of pieces to deliver checkmate—which actually rules the game a draw/tie instead of a win or a loss. Confusing, I know—but I did not make the rules!

4. Abandonment is another way to end a game of chess. And I'm only partially joking—sure, if you get angry while playing on chess.com on your iPhone you could close the app without resigning (see "2"), which would constitute defeat by abandonment, but it did happen in real life in the nineteenth century!

 Use this QR code to review the key lessons from this chapter.

CHAPTER TWO

HOW TO START THE GAME WITH THE WHITE PIECES

Please keep in mind: this is not an openings book. There are many books equal in length to this one that *only* focus on openings. My goal is to help you understand the fundamentals, and the QR codes at the end of the chapter will go into much greater detail. We had to save paper! In Chapter One we looked at how games of chess are won; now you'll need to learn how to get from the starting position to a winning position. This chapter explores the board setup and how you should start the game when you have the White pieces. Chess openings are different depending on whether you are playing White or Black because White always makes the first move.

Theoretically, you can play however you want. Playing White, you can make any legal move with one of your pieces—it can be a pawn or a knight on the first move. But it's better—and simpler—to mimic how the masters open. This is not like in other sports, where you need to be the right shape, have enough strength, or possess years of experience to copy the best. In chess, all the moves are right there and readily available to any player.

Why Learn Openings?

Have you ever gone to a restaurant where the menu was enormous? When you have tons of options to choose from and everything looks good, it can feel overwhelming. Well, chess is a little like that—except there are far more things on the menu and most of them taste terrible.

Chess openings are named after people or places—the people who played a critical role in their development or the places where they were first played or popularized. For example, on the following diagram is the Italian Opening, which is named after the seventeenth-century Italian player Gioachino Greco. A lot of the most important ideas associated with this opening can be traced back to Greco. ✐

The Sicilian Defense was born in 1813 when the English master Jacob Henry Sarratt translated an old Italian manuscript that referred to *il gioco Siciliano*—the Sicilian game. This variation of the Sicilian Defense is named after Miguel Najdorf, a twentieth-century Polish-Argentinian player who progressed the theory and ideas of this particular variation. To this day, the Najdorf Sicilian is considered the Rolls-Royce of openings for Black.

⬇ Below is the Sicilian Defense, Najdorf Variation. Some openings are called "defense" because they are named after how Black responds rather than how White plays; because White always moves first, Black is considered to be defending from the opening. A **variation** is one possible direction a game can go after the first few moves of any opening or defense are played.

Before we jump into specific advice on how to the start the game with the White pieces, think about this. At the start of the game, the board looks like this.

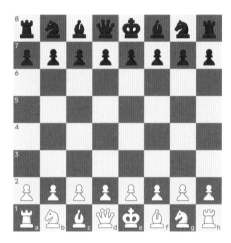

⬆ In this position, White has 20 possible first moves. All eight of the pawns can move forward either one or two squares, and each of White's knights has two available moves. In response to whichever of the 20 moves White makes, Black likewise has 20 available moves. This means that after just one move each, there are 400 possibilities of how the board could look.

Before we jump into the basics, here are some good dos and don'ts to keep in mind.

Do	Don't
Take the center	Move flank pawns or pieces to the very side of the board
Develop your pieces	Move the same piece multiple times (unless it allows you to capture material without losing any of your own pieces)
Castle your king	Move your queen out*

*If you're going for the four-move checkmate discussed on pages 18–19, then you will need to move your queen out, but as you will see, I don't recommend attempting this!

Three Principles of the Opening: Center, Develop, Castle

Highlighted in red, you can see the center of the board. ↓

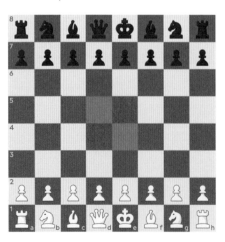

It's important to control the center because it allows your pieces to move to and see all three sides of the board. By three sides, I mean the queenside (the left side from White's perspective), the two central files (the d and e files), and the kingside (the right side from White's perspective). For example, if you put a knight on any of the four squares highlighted in red, that knight would have eight possible moves, whereas if the knight were in the very corner of the board it would only have two possible moves. If you put a bishop on any of those four squares (imagining the board is empty), it would have thirteen possible moves. Mobility is increased from the center. The more squares your pieces can move to, the more flexibility you have, the more enemy pieces you potentially can attack or pressure, and the likelier you are of strengthening the defense of your own pieces.

I'm going to show you what we call **golden moves**. These are the perfect opening moves to play if your opponent doesn't prevent you from playing them. The easiest way to learn these is to imagine that our opponent won't be moving. In a perfect world, both of your central pawns go two squares to the center of the board. ✐

 These moves are notated as e4 and d4.

 Then our knights would jump toward the center, written as Nc3 and Nf3. Finally, our bishops would move three squares each, written as Bc4 and Bf4. With our pieces set up like this, we control the center and have **developed** our knights and bishops to squares where they can attack (or "see") lots of squares. By developed, I mean we've moved our pieces—beginning with knights and bishops—from their starting squares to more active squares in the center of the board. Here they are better placed to cause problems for the opponent when we're ready to start attacking.

⬆ Next, we castle our king. White's king has slid two squares from e1 to g1, with the rook on h1 hopping over the king to f1. This is the only move in chess where you can move two pieces at once. Remember, there are a couple of conditions for castling: both the king and rook involved in castling must not have moved previously and the king cannot castle through check (i.e., the king cannot slide through a square that an enemy piece sees). Castling is important because your king is safer when tucked away on the side of the board. The notation for castling short is O-O and for castling long (i.e., toward the queenside rook) is O-O-O.

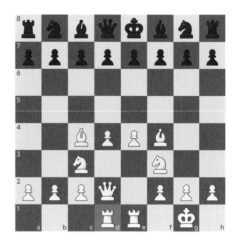

⬆ Finally, we move our queen up to d2 (Qd2), our queenside rook to d1 (Rad1), and our kingside rook to e1 (Rfe1).

These are the ten golden moves. All of our pieces are in their optimal positions, ready to advance forward as a cohesive unit. Our king is safe, every one of our pieces is defended by another piece, and we are threatening to begin a well-coordinated attack on the Black position.

However, clearly you do not get to start a game of chess with ten moves in a row, and it's your opponent's responsibility to fight back. Just as you want to control the center, so too does your opponent; just as you want to develop your pieces to the most advantageous squares, so too will your opponent be battling to occupy or control them.

e4 Openings

Let's apply the principles of the ten golden moves but with our opponent taking their turns and responding to our moves. The most common chess opening is e4, which is called the King's Pawn Opening. Since we want to start by moving our pieces toward the center, White's e pawn will move forward two squares to e4, with the goal of quickly getting two pawns in the center of the board. Black's most common response to White playing e4 on the opening move is to move a pawn to e5:

⬆ According to online chess databases, this position has been reached close to 100 million times at all levels. It's therefore the most common position at all levels of chess. Black is trying to achieve the same things as White, only a move behind. You can already see how Black's moves get in the way of our golden moves. We are no longer able to move our d pawn to d4 because Black will immediately capture it.

Instead, if Black plays e5, White might develop their knight to f3 to attack Black's e pawn.

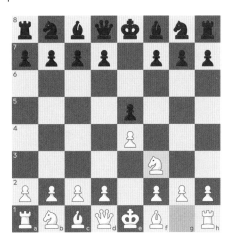

⬆ Generally White is creating the threats in the opening and Black is defending against them—that is the benefit of making the first move. At the elite level of chess, playing White is often a telling advantage because every move White makes creates threats, adds pressure, and requires a response from Black. Black is always playing catch-up.

Black might respond to Nf3 by developing their own knight to defend their e pawn and White might then develop their bishop to c4, like we see on the following page.

⬆ You may notice we've now reached the Italian Game, which we saw on page 25. Hopefully now you have a clearer sense of the logic behind the position and why it has been so popular for over four hundred years. White is looking to make those golden moves but has to anticipate Black's responses.

Alternatively, White may choose to develop their bishop to b5 instead of c4:

🖋 This is called the Ruy López or the Spanish Opening. Although the bishop is not exactly in the center of the board, it's threatening to take the Black knight on c6, which defends Black's central pawn. This is one of the most popular openings in all of chess, especially at the highest level—it was played several times at the World Chess Championship in 2021 between Magnus Carlsen and Ian Nepomniachtchi.

Of course, Black does not even have to respond with e5 when White plays e4 on the first move. This is the Sicilian Defense.

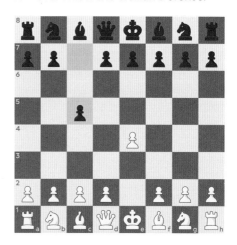

⬆ Here Black has pushed their c pawn to c5. This is another way of preventing White from playing their ideal second move of pushing the d pawn to d4. This is one of Black's most aggressive defenses.

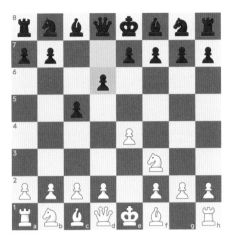

⬆ Unable to play d4, White may instead develop their knight to f3. Black may then defend their c pawn with their d pawn, like so.

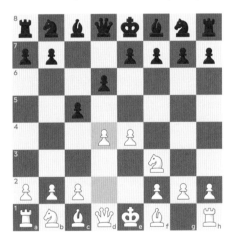

⬆ Now White might push the d pawn to d4—the difference here being that the d pawn would be defended by the White knight on f3. The queen was also protecting d4, but we don't want to bring the queen out yet.

⬆ Black may take the pawn on d4 with their c pawn, and White will recapture with their knight. White is happy with this very active knight in the center of the board—as I mentioned earlier, a knight in the center controls eight squares.

⬆ Black develops their knight to f6, threatening to capture our pawn on e4. So, we move our other knight to c3, defending the e4 pawn.

⬆ Black then moves their pawn one square to a6, preventing White from ever putting a knight or bishop on b5 (because the Black pawn could capture it)—and we've now reached the Najdorf Variation of the Sicilian Defense, which we covered on page 25. This position has been reached millions of times—more frequently by high-level players than beginners, given the complexity involved as the game develops from here. Studying openings like this will help give you a better sense of the logic behind the moves, and a clearer understanding of why some openings occur so much more frequently than others.

d4 Openings

So far we've only looked at White playing e4 on the first move. But White doesn't have to start by moving the e pawn. e4 is the most popular opening move; in fact, according to the online databases, e4 is twice as popular as d4. But d4 is by far the second most popular opening move for White. Together, e4 and d4 openings make up around 80 percent of games.

⬆ This is d4, called the Queen's Pawn Opening. This leads to a whole other subset of interesting openings for White, and like-wise different defenses from the Black side. What I always recommend to my students is not to mess around with *both* e4 and d4 openings, because you won't learn enough about either. It's better to choose an opening and play it a lot—that's the only way you'll get deeply familiar with all the complexities and nuances that arise from any opening on a chessboard.

⬆ With d4 openings, the same principles as e4 openings apply. You are still putting a pawn in the center and plan to put two pawns there. A very common response for Black is to play d5, preventing you from immediately putting your second pawn in the center—you'll notice how this mirrors the first e4/e5 position on page 29.

One of the easiest openings to learn with the White pieces is the London System, a subset of d4 openings.

⬆ After White has played d4 and Black has responded with d5, White moves their bishop to f4. We'll be looking at the London System in more detail in the second part of this book and so won't go through every move of it here. But the next diagram shows how the London System ideally looks when both sides have finished their development and castled their kings.

♟ White has developed their knights and bishops to advantageous squares and created a pyramid of pawns from the b pawn to the f pawn. Like I said, don't worry too much about how we reached this position just yet—we'll cover that later. The point is to show there are whole other branches of positions that arise from playing d4 instead of e4.

Another common d4 opening looks like this.

♟ Typically in d4 openings, the best friend of your d pawn is not your e pawn but your c pawn. This position is called the Queen's Gambit—"Queen's" because it refers to the d pawn and "gambit" because White is essentially offering Black a "free" pawn.

♚ **FUN FACT**

This is the opening the acclaimed Netflix show is named after. I would estimate that 90-95 percent of my online audience got into chess—or came back to it—because of that show, so, of course, I had to include it in this book!

✒ Black can take the pawn (called the Queen's Gambit Accepted) but then White will move their e pawn to the center, as shown in this diagram. Now White has two pawns in the center—one of our golden principles—and White's bishop attacks Black's pawn on c4. So, for the momentary loss of a pawn, White has gained great central control and quick development.

Of course, Black does not have to take the c pawn (called the Queen's Gambit Declined) and there follows a whole other subset of complicated positions. I hope you're beginning to get a sense of why it's important to choose one opening and stick to it—even the most straightforward openings have endless variations, so trying to learn both e4 and d4 openings as a beginner or intermediate player will only make things harder.

Scholar's Mate

Let's now look more closely at the four-move checkmate from the introduction (page 18), drawing on what we've learned about opening with the White pieces. Going for checkmate in four moves is obviously an aggressive approach—it also breaks some of the key principles we've talked about in this chapter, and if the opponent is prepared for it then you end up with a bad position from the opening.

I'm showing you this not because I want you to play like this—I do not believe this will benefit your understanding of the game in the long run—but because you will face this frequently when playing with the Black pieces, and it's important to know how to defend against it.

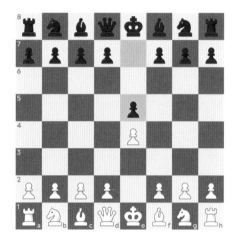

⬆ We start with our position, which has been reached 96 million times: White pawn to e4, followed by Black pawn to e5.

♟ Here White plays queen to h5, which attacks Black's pawn on e5 and sees Black's pawn on f7. The f7 pawn is important in the opening because it is the only pawn in Black's position that is *only* defended by the Black king.

There are actually two traps associated with this position. The second trap, which we will come to, is the Scholar's Mate, but first let's look at something else you might see.

♟ Here Black has made what looks like quite a natural move, pushing the g pawn to g6 and threatening to take the White queen. But Black has forgotten about defending the e5 pawn ...

White's queen takes the black pawn on e5. But it's worse than that. White's queen attacks both the Black king (which is called **check**) and the Black rook on h8. However Black defends its king, White's queen will take the Black rook on the next move, leaving White with a massive material advantage after only four moves. ✏

Let's say Black doesn't fall for the first trap, and instead Black defends the e5 pawn with the knight, as shown here. Now we are back to threatening the Scholar's Mate. ⬇

⬆ White then develops their bishop to c4, a very natural move according to the principles of our golden moves—getting our knights and bishops out to more active, attacking squares. There is now a significant threat to Black here, since White's queen and bishop both attack Black's pawn on f7.

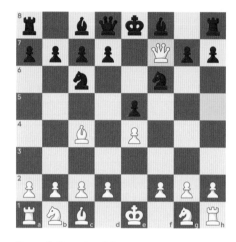

 Let's say Black makes a natural develop-ing move, bringing their knight to f6.

Queen takes f7 is **checkmate**. Black has gone down in four moves to the Scholar's Mate. In the introduction, I mentioned that this position has been reached over 600,000 times online—don't let it happen to you! ⬇

If you follow the QR code on the next page, I'll show you how to counter the Scholar's Mate in greater detail. It works until it doesn't!

> ♛ **FUN FACT**
>
> This may seem unbelievable, but nearly 30 percent of players (over 250,000) online did NOT play the checkmating move, Qxf7#. How is that even possible? They played three of the four necessary moves, and then simply got distracted. If you make it to that position, PLEASE finish the checkmate!

Summary

Longterm, aiming for the Scholar's Mate, where you reach checkmate in just four moves, is not good. Bringing your queen out on the second move won't help your position because the queen, your most valuable piece, will constantly be attacked and you'll have to waste turns moving it back to safety. Instead, you should stick to the key opening principles.

Openings are important because they teach you basic principles and set you up for success in the later stages of a chess game. Think of openings as training wheels on a bicycle or floaties in a pool—they are the necessary learning stepping-stones to improvement.

Within the first ten moves, you should control the center with one or both of your e/d pawns, develop your knights and bishops (while also targeting the center), and castle your king. Ideally, you reach the golden move setup, but in practice, both sides will fight for similar territory, so it is not always possible.

Openings that begin with e4 (King's Pawn) can lead to many different "branches," such as the Italian, Ruy López, Sicilian, French, and others. Both sides take turns sending the game into certain territory depending on the White opening and the Black defense.

However, White can also open the game with 1. d4, the second most popular first move. This can lead to the Queen's Gambit, the London, and other branches. You should choose *one* first move and play it consistently to get better at your opening of choice, rather than mixing in your games with White.

The Scholar's Mate, also known as the 4-Move Checkmate, is a way to win (or lose) a chess game almost as soon as it starts. You must remember how to both defend against it and potentially use it as a weapon against unsuspecting opponents. For your long-term chess development, I do not recommend it. But you can definitely use it to make your friends think you are the reincarnation of Bobby Fischer or the next Judit Polgár.

In Chapter Three, we'll be looking at how to defend against some of White's most common openings, and how the golden moves can be applied to playing with the Black pieces—where you are always a move behind and playing catch-up.

 Follow this QR code to review the golden moves and practice some openings with the White pieces.

CHAPTER THREE

HOW TO START THE GAME WITH THE BLACK PIECES

Now let's look at starting the game with the Black pieces. First off, a lot of what you learned in the last chapter still applies, but chess is different when you aren't the one making the first move. When playing with the Black pieces, you are responding to your opponent's opening. Nevertheless, you are still aiming for the golden moves and it's possible to get many of them on the board when playing Black, even if you are a move behind White.

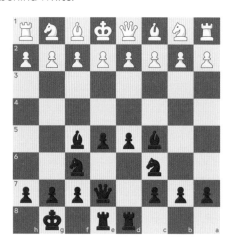

🖋 This is how the golden moves would look with Black (again imagining White hasn't made any moves). Whatever opening your opponent plays, you should still strive for pawns in the center, knights and bishops developed toward the center, castling your king, and connecting your rooks—everything we learned in the previous chapter when opening with the White pieces.

Usually, however, White will start the game with some kind of preparation, likely following a particular opening and aiming for the golden moves themselves. So with Black we are responding. This chapter will look at three different kinds of openings for Black: the traditional Black openings, which follow the principles we talked about in the previous chapter; setup-based openings with the Black pieces; and building-block openings, like the French Defense and Caro-Kann Defense.

Traditional Openings

We've talked about how—when playing with the Black pieces—we are responding to White in the opening rather than dictating the play. So-called "traditional" openings for Black mean making the most logical responses to White's moves in the opening. Let's say White plays e4 and Black responds with e5: ⬇

In the last chapter, you learned that having two pawns in the center is really important. So, Black prevents White from doing that immediately by playing e5—if White now plays d4, Black can capture the pawn. So White will likely do something else.

Instead of playing d4, White moves their knight to f3 (Nf3). Now White is attacking our pawn on e5. ↙

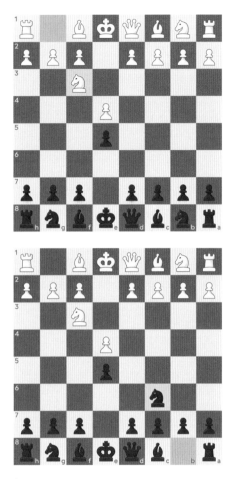

⬆ We now make a move that both protects the pawn and develops a piece toward the center by moving our knight to c6 (Nc6). White will continue to develop from here and Black will continue to respond, protecting pieces while developing your own in the most advantageous way.

In this position, White can still put a second pawn in the center but Black can capture it with the e pawn. ⬇

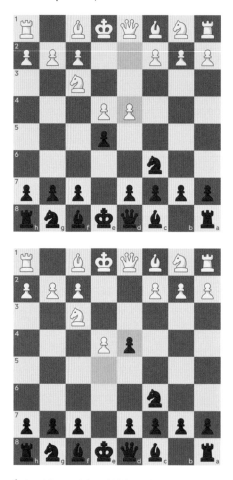

⬆ In this position, White will recapture our pawn with their knight. But the point here is that we've relieved the pressure on our position: White can no longer put two pawns in the center and from here we can develop the rest of our pieces. This is a common opening known as the Scotch, which has been played millions of times.

In this traditional opening with the Black pieces, Black is making the most logical responses to White's early threats, which simultaneously gets Black as close to the golden moves as possible. Here is an example of what the board might look like after six moves each if Black makes the most logical responses to White's moves.

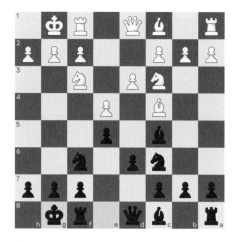

⬆ You'll notice the position is totally symmetrical. Personally, I find this way of teaching beginners very boring, not to mention impractical. Think about it: if Black copies White all the way to the end, White will deliver checkmate one move before Black and win the game!

Still, this is one of the most common opening positions; if both sides follow good opening principles and play a traditional opening, it will look something like this. As an absolute beginner this is fine, but as you start improving your game, you may choose more interesting or expansive ways to play with Black that might give you an edge in the opening if your opponent is unprepared.

Before we move on from traditional play with the Black pieces, let's look at how play might develop if White begins with d4 rather than e4:

 As with the previous position, White wants to put two pawns in the center, so Black should do something to prevent this. As with the previous example, Black puts their own pawn in the center to stop White from immediately putting their second pawn there.

In response, let's say White plays c4. This is the Queen's Gambit, which we looked at briefly in the last chapter. Black should not accept the gambit (by which I mean, Black should not capture the c4 pawn with their d5 pawn), because it's known to be an advantageous position for White. ⬇

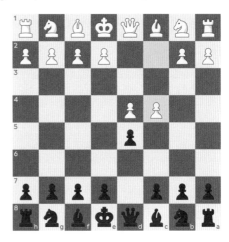

> ♚ **FUN FACT**
>
> At intermediate level, accepting the Queen's Gambit (2. …dxc4) is actually the most popular move, even though I would never recommend this move to an improving player. White's win percentage immediately jumps up to 56 percent because the position is difficult to play for Black.

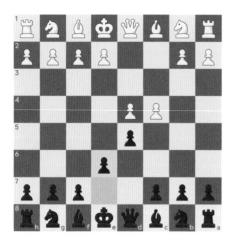

♟ Instead, Black should play e6, defending their central pawn. This would be the traditional approach, called the Queen's Gambit Declined.

Again, we are not looking at any opening in meaningful detail here just yet. My point is: when playing Black, you can get a totally acceptable position by playing the most principled responses to the way White develops in the early game. Playing the traditional way with Black will get you comfortable opening positions, but you still must react correctly to White's first few moves.

Setup-Based Openings

One of the biggest challenges when playing Black is being prepared for all the different ways White might start the game. Only a very experienced player can retain all the best responses to different White openings in sufficient depth. Setup openings, on the other hand, can be played against pretty much anything White plays. They are characterized by nearly identical piece placement and similar strategies for later in the game. Learning a "setup" has an obvious advantage: it will allow you to start the same way with Black almost all the time, so you will understand how to play it well.

One of the most common setup-based openings with the Black pieces is the King's Indian or Pirc Defense, which looks like this (from Black's perspective, the King's Indian and Pirc are the same—they just have a different name depending on White's opening move).

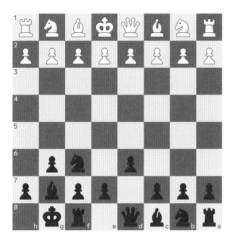

♟ Again, I've shown this without any moves from White for ease of reference. First Black develops their knight to f6, then follows a combination of four other moves—pawn to g6, bishop to g7, pawn to d6, and short castles—which gives us the position shown.

Black can play these five moves against anything White plays. And the strategy for Black from this position is quite replicable, making it easier to study and learn because the positions you find yourself in will always look broadly the same. Setup-based openings are a bit of a "cheat code" for playing Black. The drawback is that all your games may look similar, causing boredom or a lack of understanding when it comes to playing any other type of position. Setup players also can get lazy, not spotting early threats because they are absentmindedly playing the same moves over and over again.

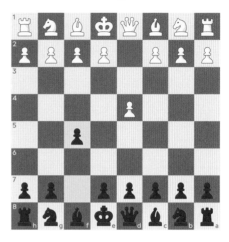

♟ Another common setup-based opening for Black is the Dutch Defense, which is when Black plays f5. Black can play this against everything White plays *except* the King's Pawn Opening, e4 (because White would be able to capture Black's pawn on f5). A Dutch Defense game might develop like this.

Both sides have developed some pieces and castled their king. Again, don't worry too much about this particular position: the point here is that the Dutch Defense allows you to play the same way against almost anything White plays, so it is another useful setup-based opening to explore in more detail if it appeals to how you want to play. ⬇

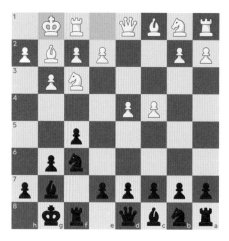

Like traditional openings for Black, setup-based openings are principled and fight for the center, although often in a more passive way than traditional openings. They have an advantage over traditional openings in that you can play them in almost all circumstances and deepen your understanding of them; the disadvantages lay in the fact that you will be mostly repeating the same positions over and over and not expanding your overall understanding of the game and knowledge of different kinds of positions.

Building-Block Openings

A building-block opening is one where you have a center presence with a pawn, but you first bolster that central pawn with another pawn defending it. The two most common building-block openings are the French Defense and the Caro-Kann. The Caro-Kann occurs when White plays e4 and Black responds with c6.

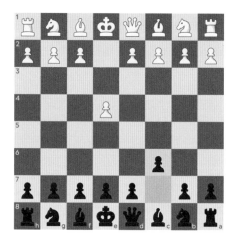

⬆ Anticipating that White will be aiming for two pawns in the center, Black uses the c pawn as a "building block." When White plays d4 on the next move . . .

♟ . . . Black plays d5. Now Black's d pawn is supported by their c pawn, so if White chose to capture it then Black could immediately recapture with their c pawn (in chess, "recapture" means capturing back a piece that has captured one of your pieces).

The French Defense is similar but Black supports their d pawn with their e pawn, as shown on the next board.

♙ Here White plays e4 but this time Black's first move is e6—the e pawn becomes the building block. Then, when White moves their d pawn to the center, Black plays d5 and again the central pawn is protected by a supporting pawn.

The Queen's Gambit Declined is another building-block opening.

 FUN FACT

According to online databases, at the 1600 and below level, responding to White's e4 with e5 (symmetrical) has been played 62 million times and scores 51 percent for White. However, Black responding with c6, the Caro-Kann Defense, has been played nearly 10 million times and drops White's win percentage to 47 percent. This shows that "mirroring" White allows White to strike first with various attacks, while the Caro-Kann catches players off guard and allows them to respond to us instead, leading to an initiative for Black.

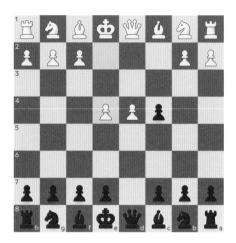

⬆ This one is slightly different because Black responds to d4 with d5—immediately putting their pawn in the center. Then after White plays c4—the gambit—Black declines taking the "free" pawn and instead supports their central pawn with e6.

You might wonder why it's best for Black to decline the Queen's Gambit. Well, think about the golden moves. What does White want? White wants two pawns in the center. If you accept the Queen's Gambit, this is the position you'll likely find yourself in:

⬆ Black is temporarily up a pawn—I say "temporarily" because White will easily win it back—but White has full control of the center and Black has completely surrendered control of the center. I'm not saying accepting the Queen's Gambit is always a losing move but this is a difficult way to play with Black and you should be aiming to control the center with pawns as much as possible.

Building-block openings provide good structure, allow Black a pawn presence in the center of the board, and give Black a good platform to develop the rest of their pieces and castle their king. Of course, if White is well prepared against any defense you choose then you'll likewise have to be prepared with the best responses. Unlike setup-based openings, any building-block opening relies on White playing a specific first move; the French Defense and Caro-Kann can only be played against e4, while the Queen's Gambit Declined can only be played against d4.

Summary

When starting the game with the Black pieces, several concepts carry over from starting with the White pieces, namely to take the center, develop, and castle; as well as sticking to certain defenses as much as possible against White's main openings. If you want to play the Caro-Kann Defense against e4, do it every game and analyze your mistakes to play better over time.

Some other things to keep in mind:
- Traditional openings are ones where you simply play by the principles we have described at length already. At times, there will be specific situations where you must know the exact response or else you will land in a worse position.
- Setup-based defenses like the King's Indian or Dutch feature more or less identical piece development and plans depending on how White opens the game. The benefit of playing setups is that you save study time and can build up a solid understanding of the position. The downside of this approach, however, is that you may find chess boring!

- Building-block defenses attempt to occupy the center with a pawn—just like our opponent playing with the White pieces—and support it with another pawn. The Caro-Kann, French, and Queen's Gambit Declined are all excellent choices to adopt into your repertoire if you choose to take this approach.

The point of this chapter has not been to cover every opening with the Black pieces—far from it. I haven't covered the Sicilian Defense, for example, one of the most popular defenses at the grandmaster level. That's because it's a bit too complicated for beginners. Likewise, there are many other openings for the Black pieces that I haven't mentioned. This chapter explored what it means to play with Black and demonstrates the underlying principles of some of Black's most common responses to openings with the White pieces.

Follow the QR code to explore some Black openings in more detail.

CHAPTER FOUR
ENDGAMES I

Now that we have explored the basics of the opening with both White and Black, the next three chapters will introduce you to endgames. The endgame is defined as the last stage of a chess game, where there are just a few pieces remaining. In this chapter, we will learn how to checkmate with the minimum number of pieces on the board to do so, which is 3 or 4. You will need to learn how to deliver these checkmates, because simply achieving a winning position does not automatically grant you victory—you must know how to finish off the game.

Ladder Mate

The easier type of checkmate to learn is the Ladder Mate, which occurs when you have two very powerful pieces and you walk the enemy king to the edge of the board, where it has no escape. It's called the "ladder" checkmate because it involves a series of checks, each like the rung of a ladder—and every rung brings you closer to checkmate.

A Ladder Mate requires two pieces that can attack both vertically and horizontally—in this example we have two queens, but it could be a rook and a queen or two rooks. (Remember:

having two queens is made possible by promoting a pawn, which we discussed on page 6.)

↟ Here White's queen on g8 attacks Black's king, while the second queen on f7 "cuts off" the Black king's escape to the next rank. With no square to escape to, the Black king is checkmated. The key to delivering Ladder Mate is forcing the enemy king to any of the outermost ranks (the 1st or 8th ranks) *or* the outermost files (the a or h file). It doesn't matter which rank or file you use, so long as it's the very edge of the board; that way, the enemy king has nowhere left to run when you deliver your final check.

You can also deliver a Ladder Mate vertically, like in this example.

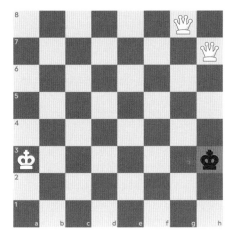

♟ The same principle applies: one of our pieces is cutting off the Black king's escape and the other is delivering checkmate.

But how do we get there? Your opponent is not going to walk into a Ladder Mate voluntarily. Imagine we have a position like this one:

♟ To achieve a ladder checkmate from this position, we must force the Black king to the outmost files or ranks. From this position, White's goal will be to push the Black king down to the first rank of the board (the quickest Ladder Mate in this position would actually be by forcing the Black king to the a file, but let's choose the 1st rank so we can see the technique in more detail). You can force the enemy king to whichever outer rank or file you like when delivering Ladder Mate, but it makes sense to choose the rank or file the enemy king is closest to.

First, White will move the queen that is farthest from the Black king. We want to leave the queen on e6 where it is for now, since it's cutting off the Black king from moving up the board—remember, our goal is to force the enemy king down to the 1st rank, so we don't want to allow the king any opportunity to escape up the board.

⬆ Once the queen moves from f7 to f5, it is checking the Black king. The White queen on e6 covers the entire 6th rank, so the enemy king is forced to travel down to the 4th rank instead.

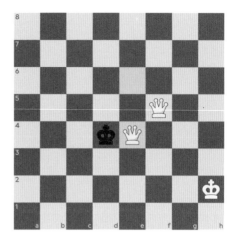

⬆ But now our "distant" queen yet again delivers a check. The two White queens alternate attacks, essentially "climbing a ladder" down the board together. The queen we moved on the last turn now cuts off the Black king, again forcing the Black king downward. Continue this technique until the Black king runs out of board and it will be checkmate.

You'll find a QR code at the end of the chapter to practice this technique. Ladder Mate is easiest with two queens but is possible with a queen and rook or two rooks. There is an important difference if a rook is involved, though. Remember that rooks do not defend each other diagonally, whereas queens do. Look at the next position:

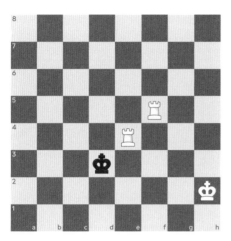

⬆ It looks like White is doing everything right. One rook is cutting off the Black king and the other rook will move to f3 and check the Black king. But if White plays rook to f3 in this position . . . ⬇

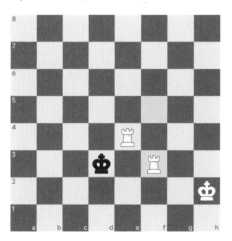

. . . the Black king will simply capture the rook on e4! ✎

It's still possible to checkmate Black with one White rook and the White king, but it will require a different technique, one that's trickier than the Ladder Mate. So be careful of this.

When attempting the Ladder Mate with two rooks, you need to keep the rooks as far away from the opposing king as possible, like in this example. ⬇

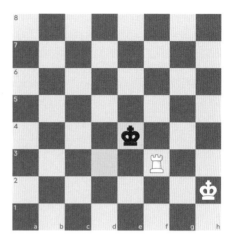

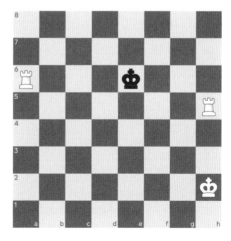

The principle is the same but the White rooks are safe from the Black king. In situations like this, it often means using one of your turns to slide a rook from one side of the board to the other. When using rooks to deliver Ladder Mate, you need to keep them farther away from the enemy king; unlike queens, the enemy king can approach and capture your rooks if you let it get too close.

As with the Ladder Mate with queens, use the QR code at the end of the chapter to practice Ladder Mates with rooks. Ladder Mate is the easiest checkmate to know and the easiest to practice.

King and Queen Mate

This is a checkmate you have to know. The King and Queen Mate is a winning position you could often find yourself in at the end of a game but you need to know the technique—which is not too tricky to learn. You should be able to deliver this checkmate without giving a single check along the way (until checkmate, that is). That's a rule to keep in mind. Another thing to keep in mind with the King and Queen Mate is that—like the Ladder Mate—the goal is to push the opposing king to any outer edge of the board. There is a specific technique for doing this.

Let's take the next position.

⬆ White has reached the endgame and is up a queen. This should be a win for White 100 percent of the time. But to deliver the King and Queen Mate, you need to know the technique; otherwise the Black king will simply run around the board while you give aimless checks.

 FUN FACT

When played perfectly, most king and queen checkmates are forced within 7 to 8 moves (by the attacking side). From the worst possible starting position, a King and Queen Mate can still be forced in a maximum of 10 moves. But don't worry—as long as you don't break the 50-move rule (page 83) then you can take as many moves as you need!

The technique here is called **knight opposition:**

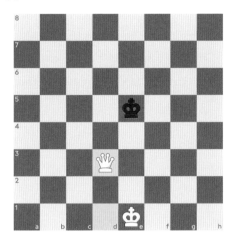

⬆ To chase the Black king to the edge of the board, you need to move your queen to a square where—if your queen were a knight—it would be checking the Black king. Chasing the opposing king in this way cuts off its escape routes and will gradually force it into a corner. Knight opposition keeps your queen a safe distance from the enemy king and restricts the enemy king's movement; it cannot cross the rank or file the queen occupies, so you are boxing in the enemy king and the box gets smaller with every move.

⬇ If the Black king moves up one square...

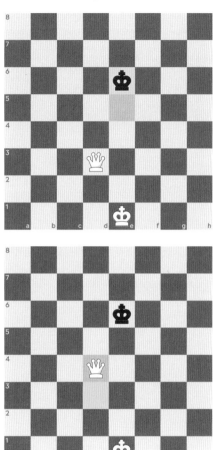

⬆ ... you copy the king, moving your queen up one square—always remaining in that knight opposition. If the king goes one square backward, your queen goes one square backward. If the king goes one square diagonally, your queen goes one square diagonally.

You do this until the opposing king is forced into the corner.

🡙 If you have remained in knight opposition with your queen, you should find the opposing king will be stuck in the corner and only have two available squares, with no choice but to shuffle backward and forward between them. But be very careful here! You *must* leave the opposing king with two safe squares to move between—do not move your queen again in the position shown here.

If you put your queen in knight opposition of the opposing king in the very corner of the board, you've taken away all available squares for the Black king to move to. It isn't check, which means the game ends in stalemate and a draw (we'll look at stalemates more in Chapter Six). 🖎

Instead, when the opposing king is trapped in the corner with at least two squares to move between (in this example, Black's king shuffles between the h7 and h8 squares), it's time to march our own king up the board.

🡙 In this position, while the Black king shuffles between its two corner squares, we walk our own king all the way to the f6 square . . .

... and only then do we play the first check in the entire sequence, attacking the Black king in the corner with our queen, which is now defended by our king. This is checkmate. ⬇

That's the technique for checkmating with a queen and king. Remember three key points here: there should be no checks along the way (checks won't mean you lose but they're a waste of time, as the knight opposition technique is most effective); you should chase the opposing king into the corner by using knight opposition with your queen; and make sure you give the opposing king at least two squares to move between in the corner, since otherwise it will be a stalemate.

King and Rook Mate

For checkmate using the rook and king, the technique is different than using a queen and king. Let's take this position.

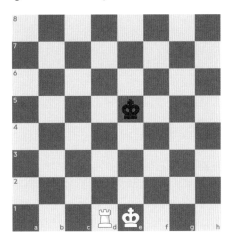

⬆ Checkmating with a rook and king requires much more involvement from your own king. Your king has to help along the way—unlike a queen, a rook cannot trap an opposing king in the corner on its own.

As with the King and Queen Mate, we need to force the opposing king to any edge of the board. Before we go through the technique, below is how a typical King and Rook Mate looks:

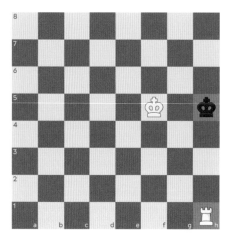

✏ Let's imagine we've just moved our king from d3 to d4. This is the position we want. Our king is in knight opposition with Black's king, while our rook stops the Black king from crossing the e file. The purpose of this is to eventually force the Black king into coming into direct opposition with our own king, as we see here.

🔖 We have forced the black king to the side of the board and delivered checkmate with our rook. It's checkmate because our own king covers all the Black king's escape squares. But how do we get here?

To get here, we're going to use knight opposition again, but this time we'll be putting our own king in knight opposition to the opponent's king, while our rook cuts off the black king either vertically or horizontally.

🔖 This diagram shows what I mean by "direct opposition." The kings face each other with one empty square between them. When Black plays the move that puts their king into this position (for example, let's say Black just moved their king from f3 to f4), it's time to play a check with our rook . . .

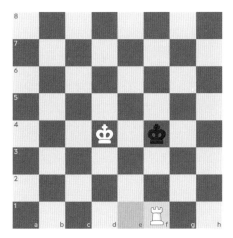

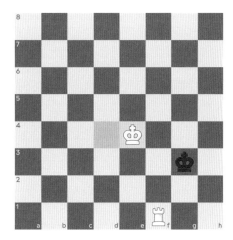

⬆ You'll notice this is similar to the final checkmating position we're aiming for, only in this case not at the very edge of the board.

But we've reduced the Black king's options—it can now move only to the g file, as we see here. ⬇

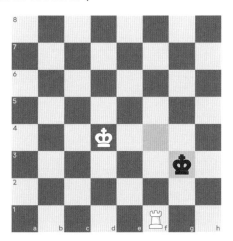

⬆ Now we move our king to the e file, as shown here. Remember that we want our king in knight opposition until the Black king is forced to move their king into opposition with our own. If *we* play into king opposition (i.e., if we make the move that leaves the two kings facing each other with a single empty square between them), Black will use their turn to move out of it (either up or down) and we won't be able to play the crucial rook check that pushes the Black king toward the outer rank or file we need to deliver checkmate.

This one is trickier than the King and Queen Mate but it is forced—meaning if you follow this technique then the opponent cannot escape eventual checkmate. If the opponent knows what they're doing, they won't walk into king opposition. They might use their king to attack your rook, as we see here.

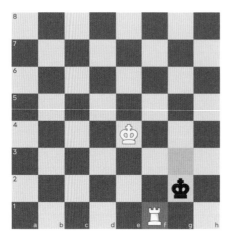

↑ If this happens, simply move your rook all the way up the file to the opposite end of the board and continue looking for knight opposition with your own king. Remember, knight opposition means a position where our king would be checking the enemy king if our king were a knight.

And remember, if you see that your opponent will be forced to move into king opposition on their next move, don't move your king! Simply move your rook somewhere (stay on the same rank or file so you're still cutting off the enemy king). Essentially, you should waste a move so that your opponent will have to play into your hands on the next move, after which you play your check and force it another step closer to checkmate on the edge of the board.

Summary

Learning the techniques for the Ladder, King and Queen, and King and Rook checkmates is very important because if you find yourself in one of those positions, you should always win. But without knowing the techniques you'll end up chasing the opposing king around the board until you end up drawing, either because of time, stalemate, or agreeing to a draw because it's hopeless.

You should be aware that king and queen, king and rook, and king and pawn are the only winning endgames when you have only one piece plus your king. If you have a king and a bishop versus a king, that's a draw. It's impossible to checkmate the opposing king with just a bishop and a king. The same is true for a king and a knight; in fact, even if you have a king and *two* knights versus just a king, it's still a draw. These are impossible because the pieces cannot combine to trap an enemy king—they simply don't cover enough squares between them.

Ladder checkmate is the most efficient means of winning a game when there are few pieces remaining. You can use a combination of two queens, two rooks, or one each. You will slowly push the enemy king across the board, alternating the movements of your pieces to ensure a smooth victory on the edge of the board. (Be careful about stalemates and the enemy king capturing one of your rooks!)

The King and Queen and the King and Rook checkmates are essential to graduating from beginner to intermediate, similar to breaking the piece of wood in martial arts to receive the next color belt (is that really a thing, or just something you see in movies?). Be sure to memorize the knight opposition technique and copycat method to push the defending king to the corner of the board.

Throughout this chapter, we have learned how to win three very common endgames where the opposing king stands alone. But as you will come to realize, few chess games make it to such a barren position. Checkmate frequently occurs with many pieces scattered across the board, even if the opposing king has an entire army of pieces surrounding it. For example, take the absurd position at right. ✐

That is checkmate. In this position Black is up 59 points of material, which is incredible, because each side starts with only 39 points' worth of material! But Black has somehow managed to promote four pawns into four extra queens. Material is very important in chess, but in the end, nothing matters

except checkmate, and in this position White's knight checkmates the Black king in the corner.

The game doesn't end even if you are up 59 points of material. The game ends with checkmate. This ties in with what we learned in this chapter about converting material advantages into wins with the correct technique; it also sets up our next chapter, where we'll be looking at checkmates that can occur when there are many more pieces on the board during the middlegame.

Follow this QR code to practice the Ladder Mate, King and Queen Mate, and King and Rook Mate.

CHAPTER FIVE
ENDGAMES II

In the previous chapter, we looked at check-mating techniques you'll need to know at the very end of the game to convert a winning position into a win. In this chapter, we're going to look at checkmates that can occur in the middlegame, when there are many more pieces on the board. Remember, opportunities to deliver checkmate can present themselves at any stage of the game—even three or four moves in, as we saw in earlier chapters. You should always be looking for checkmate, even when there are many pieces on the board.

Solo Acts

There are certain situations in chess where one piece on its own can deliver the fatal blow of checkmate. These are called "solo acts."

The first solo-act checkmate I want to cover is Back-Rank Mate, which typically occurs when a castled king is blocked in by its own pawns on the 1st or 8th rank of the board:

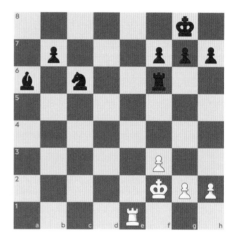

↥ You can see in this position that the Black king would need two moves to get off the 8th rank. Black's own pawns block the king's immediate escape route from the back rank. White is trailing by 7 points of material in this position but has checkmate in one . . .

. . . by moving the rook from e1 to e8. White's rook attacks Black's king horizontally and the king has no escape, nor can any of Black's pieces block or capture the rook. The Back-Rank Mate can be delivered by a queen, too, since it's the other piece besides a rook that attacks horizontally. ⬇

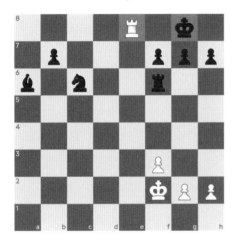

This is the simplest example of a Back-Rank Mate. Always be looking for any positions where the opposing king is trapped on the back rank by their own pawns or pieces, because the opportunity for Back-Rank Mate arises more than you might think. I'm showing you this not just as an attacking weapon but also a warning: make sure your own king is never left trapped and defenseless like this. The easiest way to do this is to make a *luft*—an escape square—for your king, typically by moving one of the pawns on the rank in front of your castled king. We'll come onto this in more detail later on, but for now make sure you're always looking for Back-Rank Mate opportunities and make sure your own king has somewhere to run if it's attacked by a rook or queen on the back rank.

I've shown you the most typical version of a Back-Rank Mate, but there's a special example you should also be aware of involving the queen.

⬆ Even though Black looks to have an escape square off the back rank (the g7 square), this is checkmate. That's because the queen attacks horizontally and diagonally. If the queen were a rook in this position, the Black king could run to g7 and it wouldn't be mate. Keep an eye out for this from both an attacking and defending standpoint!

Both of these scenarios are examples of something called **forced checkmate**. A forced checkmate is a position in which, if you play the correct moves, checkmate is unavoidable for the enemy king. In these examples, White only has to play one correct move. Other forced checkmates can be two, three, or any number of moves that, if all the correct moves are found, means checkmate is unavoidable.

Another solo-act checkmate is the Fool's Mate, which we looked at in Chapter Two. Fool's Mate is a diagonal, solo-act checkmate, where just the queen delivers mate on its own. In the diagram below, we see the Black queen attacking the White king from the h4 square. The White king has nowhere safe to run, nor can any other White pieces block or capture the Black queen.

🖋 This is a diagonal attack from one piece and is completely unstoppable. Unlike Back-Rank Mate, achieving this position is extremely rare because your opponent would have to begin the game with two very bad and illogical moves.

For a diagonal checkmate to happen, the king has to be completely crowded in by its own pieces, with none of those pieces able to capture the attacking piece or block the attack. Here is another example of a diagonal checkmate, this time with a White bishop doing the attacking.

⬆ The Black king is stranded in the corner and—despite being surrounded by its pieces—none of them can fight off the attacking bishop. Again, this is a pretty unlikely position to find oneself in, but it's worth illustrating the point that diagonally attacking pieces can deliver solo-act checkmates just like horizontally attacking pieces can.

Solo-act checkmates don't require help from any other pieces, though they do rely on help from your opponent. In Back-Rank Mate, your opponent needs to leave their king trapped and unguarded on the back rank. In the Fool's Mate and other diagonal mates, your opponent's king will need to be suffocated by its own pieces.

The last solo-act checkmate I want to show you is the Smothered Mate, which is the funniest one. An L-shaped checkmate via the knight happens pretty rarely so it is considered pretty exciting and epic to get in a game.

see the Black king here has been failed by its own pieces—they got way too close and didn't leave it enough breathing room, which has allowed the White knight, galloping solo, to deliver checkmate.

In most solo-act checkmates, the opposing king hasn't been looked after by its own pieces. They've either abandoned the king on the back rank, left it terribly guarded, or smothered it to death in the corner. Essentially, most solo-act checkmates require poor play from your opponent—but you should always be looking for them, because you'll be amazed how often the opportunities come up at the beginner and even intermediate level.

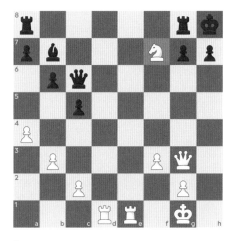

♟ Similar to other solo-act checkmates, your opponent needs to do some things wrong to end up in this situation. With the Back-Rank and diagonal checkmates, the king might not necessarily be completely boxed in; with Smothered Mate, the king literally needs to be smothered by its own pieces for it to work, as shown in the diagram. You can

 FUN FACT

According to Chess.com's Puzzles stats, I have only solved 76 percent of my Smothered Checkmate positions correctly. My parents would not have been happy with a "C" on my school report card, and I am not happy with a "C" on my puzzle skills. I need to practice more!

Two-Piece Checkmate

While one-piece checkmates are possible, as we've seen, more often than not you'll need more than one piece to deliver checkmate. It's much more nuanced, sophisticated, and necessary to learn how your pieces can work together to checkmate an enemy king when the opposing defense is better than what we saw in the examples in the last section. In this section we're going to look at some examples of checkmates where two of your pieces coordinate to deliver the fatal blow.

The most common two-piece checkmates involve the queen, typically with the queen delivering mate while being protected by another piece. Take this position as an example.

✒ There are a couple of things at play here. First of all, you'll notice that both sides have made a *luft* for their king by moving out one pawn each (the pawns on h3 and h6), so neither king is in any danger of getting Back-Rank Mated. Therefore, it's likely we're going to need to coordinate two of our pieces to deliver checkmate in this position. Now look at White's queen and bishop. They are positioned in something called a **battery**, which is when two strong pieces are arranged on the same diagonal, rank, or file with the piece in front able to attack enemy pieces while being defended by the piece behind it. In this example, we have a battery of our queen and bishop, but batteries can also be formed with a queen and rook, two rooks, or even two queens if a player has managed to promote a pawn to a second queen.

The battery in this position is particularly powerful because the queen and bishop are aligned to attack Black's g7 pawn.

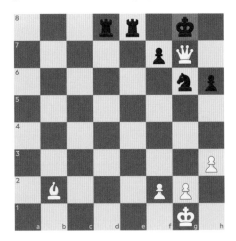

♦ When the queen captures the g7 pawn, it's checkmate. Only the Black king is defending that pawn and because White's bishop protects the queen, the Black king cannot capture the White queen. Likewise, the Black king has nowhere to run because the White queen covers all the escape squares. A queen combining with a bishop is one of the most common two-piece checkmates.

↑ You might remember the Scholar's Mate position (see page 35) in Chapter Two, where the queen and bishop combined to deliver checkmate. While not a battery, the principle is the same: the White queen crashes into the Black position and cannot be captured by the king because the bishop defends.

It's important, therefore, to remember that the bishop doesn't have to be supporting the queen via a battery as we saw in the previous example. The pieces don't have to be arranged in a battery to coordinate in a checkmating attack—they can come in from totally different directions as long as they are threatening the same square in the Black position.

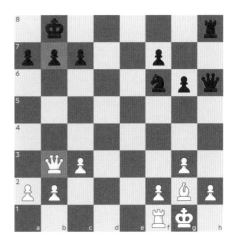

↑ Here is another example of a queen and bishop combining to threaten mate. Here the White queen and bishop attack the b7 pawn from different angles. When White plays the queen to take b7 . . .

. . . it's checkmate. Even though the queen and bishop didn't start on the same diagonal, they end on the same diagonal. White's bishop on g2 prevents the Black king from capturing the White queen, and the Black king has nowhere safe to run. ↓

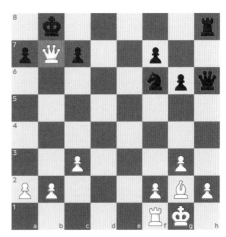

There's a bonus consideration in this position, too. Look at Black's queen and rook on the h file. This is also a battery, aimed right at White's h2 pawn! If it had been Black's turn instead of White's, Black would have checkmated first by playing queen takes h2:

↑ You can see here how effectively a queen also forms a battery with a rook. As with queen and bishop, a queen and rook can also combine from different angles to deliver a checkmate, for example one attacking horizontally and the other vertically.

The queen can also combine with a knight to deliver mate. Let's go back to the White queen and bishop battery position, only this time we're removing the bishop:

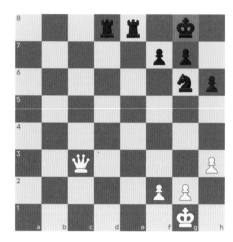

↑ Let's try something different. Imagine you can place a White knight anywhere on the board before making your next move. Where would you put the knight so that it combines with our queen on c3 to deliver checkmate?

There are actually two correct answers. A knight on either f5 or h5, as shown in the next two boards, would protect our queen and combine to deliver checkmate. In each case, the White queen attacks the Black king. The Black king cannot safely escape, nor can it capture the White queen, because it's defended by the White knight on either f5 or h5. ✒

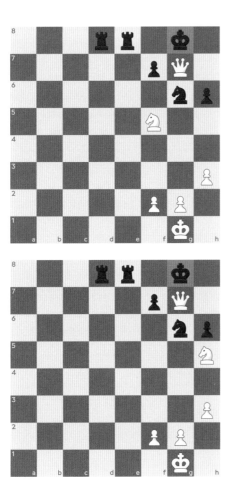

It looks like a knight on e6 would also protect our White queen, but it wouldn't be safe—both Black's rook on e8 and pawn on f7 would be able to capture it. Now let's take the position below, again with the White bishop removed:

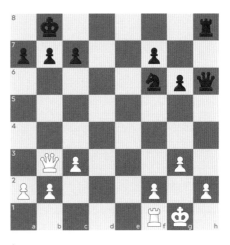

♟ Once again, let's imagine that White has the power to choose where to place a knight. Where would you place it?

There are two answers—a5 or c5, as shown here. In each scenario, the knight protects the queen when it captures the Black pawn on b7, meaning the Black king has nowhere to run and cannot capture the White queen. ⬇

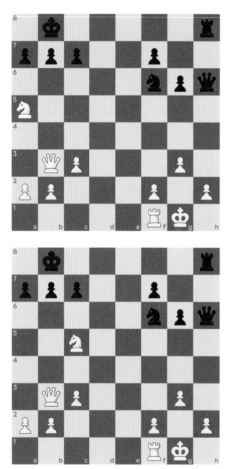

Hopefully that helps give you an understanding of how the queen can combine with other pieces to deliver checkmate. Typically, these combinations work best when the queen goes first, defended by a lesser piece, but there are situations where other pieces deliver the fatal strike, defended by the queen. Follow the QR code at the end of the chapter (page 75) to practice some of these checkmates.

So far, the two-piece mates we've looked at have all involved the queen. But other pieces can combine, too, as shown in this diagram.

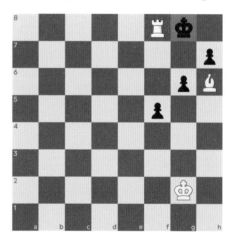

⬆ Here White's rook and bishop combine to checkmate the Black king. The bishop is defending the rook, which attacks the enemy king on the back rank. Between those two White pieces, all of Black's possible escape squares are covered.

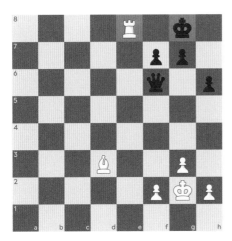

⬆ Another common way in which a rook and bishop combine to deliver mate is shown here.

You'll see in this position that—while the White bishop isn't directly involved in the checkmate—it's still playing a pivotal role. Oftentimes a bishop can cover the *luft* of an enemy king, preventing the king from escaping when the rook attacks it on the back rank. This is a different kind of Back-Rank Mate, and definitely one to look out for in your games!

Though rarer, a bishop and knight can also combine to deliver checkmate:

⬆ Here the White knight attacks the Black king and the White bishop covers the escape squares on g7 and h8.

Taking Checkmates to the Next Level

Now it's time to add another layer of complexity to some of the things we've looked at in this chapter. Let's start with this position.

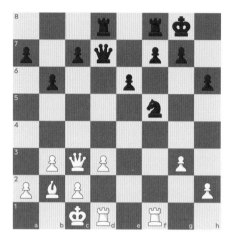

↑ Hopefully the first thing you notice about this position is that White has a queen and bishop battery lined up on Black's g7 pawn. But be careful: if the queen takes the pawn in this position, Black's knight on f5 will simply capture the queen.

So, what should White do in this position? To win here, White needs to use a concept called **removing the defender**. This is when you attack or capture a piece that is otherwise preventing you from delivering checkmate or winning material—in this case, Black's knight. With that in mind, White's best move here is taking that knight on f5 with the rook, as we see here:

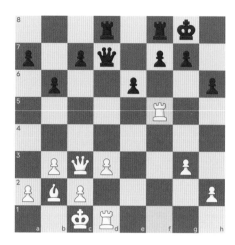

↑ Under normal circumstances, this is a really bad decision because a rook is worth 5 points and a knight is worth 3. But if Black recaptures the White rook with their e6 pawn . . .

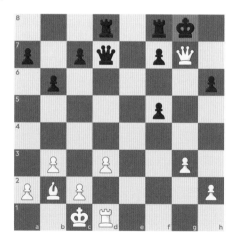

↑ . . . White is now be able to deliver mate with the queen on g7. This expands on everything we've learned in this chapter, showing how you need to see checkmating opportunities in advance and come up with ways to get there.

More often than not, Black will have pieces defending their weak points so there won't always be a single checkmating move on the board. But adding this layer of removing the defender will pave the way for more checkmating attacks. In the previous example, trading a rook for a knight traditionally would be considered "bad chess," but here it's the winning move—the stronger you get at chess, the more you'll understand how and when to temporarily sacrifice material to win games.

To improve your checkmating, you should practice training positions that involve forced checkmates. Remember, a forced checkmate is a solved position—oftentimes coming from real games—in which, if you play the correct moves, checkmate is unavoidable for the enemy king. Start by practicing checkmates in one (like Back-Rank Mates) before practicing checkmates in two moves, three moves, and so on. As you improve your one-move checkmates, you'll begin to identify how to get into positions to deliver those checkmates, which is the key to checkmates in two or more moves. Sometimes, when thinking about how to checkmate an enemy king, it's worth imagining what you would do if you had two, three, or four moves in a row. Then try to get those moves on the board, aiming for them to be as forcing as possible; that is, making moves that require a predictable response from your opponent, like checks or attacking high-value enemy pieces.

Checkmates in more than one move are forced sequences of moves, typically checks on the enemy king that force it into predictable moves; remember, your opponent must respond to check by moving or defending their king, hence why their moves are predictable. Let's look at an example of a checkmate in two by force:

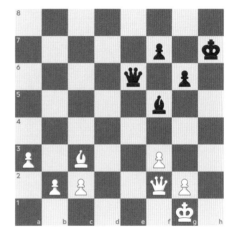

♟ Can you solve it? See how the White bishop on c3 is like a laser beam narrowly missing the Black king. If we could pick up the White queen and place it on h8, it would be checkmate. That would be illegal, obviously, so how do we get there while ensuring Black has no way to stop it? We play a check by moving the queen to h4 . . .

... In response to this, the Black king has only one legal move ... ⬇

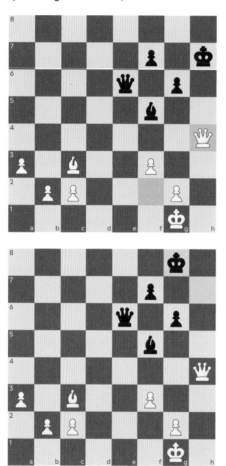

🔼 ... which is moving to g8. Now, just as we wanted, the White queen and bishop both see the h8 square ...

🔼 ... and the queen slides down to h8 to deliver checkmate, protected by the bishop.

This is an example of a forced checkmate in two moves. The better you get at identifying and exploiting weaknesses near your opponent's king, the better you will become as a chess player. Not all your checkmates will happen in the first four moves, and not all your checkmates will happen on the back rank. But once you learn to coordinate your pieces in an effective way, you'll really be starting to understand what chess is all about. Not all checkmates will just appear on the board as a one-move win; you have to hone your ability to see checkmates two, three, or more moves out and make forcing moves (like checks) to get there.

Summary

While it is important to know the techniques of endgame checkmates—which we learned in Chapter Four—most checkmates usually occur in the middlegame.

"Solo-act" checkmates, as I like to call them, feature just one attacking piece against a king. The most common type of solo-act checkmate is the back rank, where a king gets abandoned by his fellow pieces and has no escape against a lateral attacker, such as a queen or rook. Additionally, a knight can deliver a smothered checkmate, while a queen or a bishop will occasionally win on a diagonal.

Two-piece checkmates are the most likely to occur in your games as they feature some of the most natural coordination between your pieces. Frequently, a queen cannot deal damage alone, but the support of a bishop or a knight can help, especially when the two pieces have sights on the same square.

There are also checkmates where the escape is monitored by one of our secondary pieces. We saw an example where our two aggressors were technically not looking at the same side of the board, but coordinated beautifully to prevent the enemy king from getting out of danger.

In "forced checkmate" positions involving more than one move, the correct sequence of moves will always lead to a victory for one side, usually via a series of checks. Regardless of how many defensive moves exist, the attacking side will always deliver a checkmate (if played accurately).

To improve your vision of spotting checkmates in one, two, or three moves, I recommend solving puzzles. There are millions of checkmate puzzles waiting to be solved, both in print and online resources.

Follow this QR code to practice some checkmating puzzles.

CHAPTER SIX

ENDGAMES III

In this chapter we're going to cover draws. We've almost exclusively looked at winning and losing in the last few chapters, but it's important to look at the ways in which a game of chess is drawn, what you have to know about the different methods for drawing, and when you should be playing for a draw (basically when you're dead lost and want to salvage a tie). Obviously, this book isn't called *How to Draw at Chess* but it's something you need to be aware of—a draw might be the best result you can get from a losing position, and you also need to be wary of the tricks an opponent may use to try to draw a game when you have a winning advantage.

A draw is a tie. There are a few ways in which there is no winner in a game of chess. If one point is up for grabs in a tournament, each player gets a half point in the event of a tie. In this chapter we're going to cover all the serious (and some goofy) examples of how to draw a game of chess, particularly looking at situations where you should strive for a

draw from a losing position. Think about it like a soccer match: if you're down 3–0 at half-time, a 3–3 tie at the end of the match would be a great result. Of course you want to win all your games of chess, but since that isn't possible, learning how to make draws out of bad situations is a crucial skill.

If you pit two chess supercomputers—for example, Stockfish and Komodo—against one another in a 100-game match, with matching technical aspects and server sizes, it wouldn't be a surprise if they made 100 draws. That's because chess played perfectly is a draw. This is why in the Computer Chess Championship, the engines play two games in each of a variety of predetermined starting positions and openings, which provides imbalance and opportunities for wins.

Humans, clearly, are anything but perfect. You're not perfect. I, with a peak rating of 2430 and an International Master, still make plenty of mistakes on the chessboard. For humans, chess is nowhere near solved, which is part of what makes it so fascinating, and one of the reasons you're holding this book, wanting to learn more about the game—particularly how to make fewer blunders and win more than you lose.

The fun fact on this page should show you how imperfect chess is at the beginner and intermediate level. Players are messing up a lot, and clearly there aren't enough players out there who know how to rescue draws from dead-lost positions. Let's now take a look at the different ways to draw a game of chess.

Draw by Agreement

The first scenario we're going to look at is when players agree to a draw. Why would they do this? Well, for example, look at the position below:

♟ After a long, hard-fought battle, two players settle for a draw in this position. One player offers a draw; the other player accepts. Theoretically you are free to offer a draw on move two—it's just that your opponent doesn't have to accept. In this case, it's a totally equal position and—with best play—this is a draw. If I showed this position to 100 grandmasters, every single one would accept a draw offer in this position against a player of similar strength—whether they have the White pieces or Black.

That is because material is equal, the pawns are symmetrical, and the only way to win would be if your opponent made a horrendous mistake, which wouldn't happen at the master level. Of course, if this were a timed

---

♔ **FUN FACT**

Of the 2.4 million master games recorded on the Lichess database, 43 percent end in draws. White wins 33 percent of the time, Black wins 24 percent of the time, and the rest—the predominant result—are draws (ties). However, if I change the sample to look at nonmaster games (i.e., games played by normal people on Lichess with an average rating of 1600), out of a sample size of 220 million only 4 percent of games end in draws. Just 4 percent! White wins 50 percent of the time and Black wins 46 percent of the time. That is nuts.

match and Black had three seconds left on the clock versus thirty seconds for White, more likely than not White would try to win on time. But in a long game, if both players have sufficient time, the players would agree to a draw here. Grandmasters would shake hands, analyze the game, and go and get a drink together.

In the last round of the 2022 Chess Olympiad, this was a position that came up between Spanish grandmaster Jaime Santos Latasa (playing White) and grandmaster Robert Hovhannisyan of Armenia (playing Black):

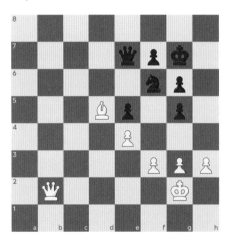

♟ After 69 moves of play, Black played knight to f6 and the players agreed to a draw. This isn't as balanced a position as the previous example; while material is equal, Black has a knight versus a bishop for White, and the pawn structures are different. However, players at the highest level have a mutual understanding of the fact that neither player can turn this into a win. Both sides are too solid and the overwhelming risk you'd have to take to try to win this position would probably backfire. So, agreeing to a draw makes sense here.

Draw agreement has actually become a controversial subject at the top level of chess because in no other sport can you agree to a draw. Even in soccer—one of the only major sports that allow matches to end in ties, apart from championship matches where there has to be a winner—the two sides cannot get midway through the game, agree to a draw, and head for an early shower. As interest and prize purses have increased in chess, sponsors and fans alike have expressed frustration with games where the players play for thirty minutes (or less), get bored, and shake hands on a tie.

In a tournament in Sofia, Bulgaria, in 2005, the rule for offering a draw was removed, meaning if players wanted a draw they'd have to look for other means—which we'll come to in the following sections. That rule was implemented in order to prolong the games and lead to more combative play and more decisive results. Often at the highest level masters can play too safe, particularly with the Black pieces, where a draw is often a great result. As you can tell from the draw statistics we looked at earlier, beginners and intermediate players do not need the Sofia rule because 96 percent of the time they play to the death anyway.

Draw by Repetition

Threefold repetition or threefold position is when you and your opponent shuffle back and forth in a way that either you repeat the exact same sequences of moves three times in a row, or you somehow get to the exact same position three times. And the same position occurring three times doesn't necessarily have to be in a row. Let's look at an example of threefold repetition:

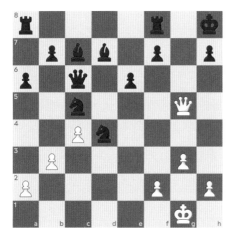

⬆ In this position, White is down 21 points of material, which is very bad. Hopefully this book will help you avoid ever being down this much material in a game. But, bizarrely, White isn't losing here—a chess computer would say that this is an equal position. That's because White can deliver threefold repetition and in doing so secure a draw.

White's queen moves to f6, which gives a check. The Black king has only one move to escape the check . . . ⬇

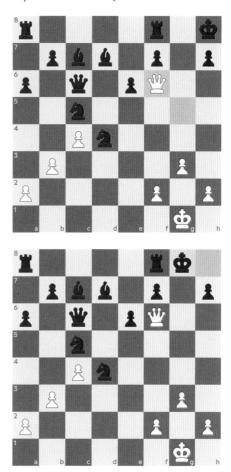

⬆ . . . which is moving to g8. Then White plays another check, returning to the g5 square . . .

... and again Black has only one legal move, returning to the h8 square in the corner. When White does this three times, the game is declared a draw, and White doesn't lose despite being down 21 points of material. This is a very important thing to be aware of when you're in a terrible position; likewise it's something you need to be aware of if you're winning—try to make sure your opponent can't salvage a draw by playing perpetual checks.

The rule around threefold repetition was introduced for situations exactly like this. If this rule weren't in place, White would repeat the same moves forever until somebody lost on time or a player lost the will to go on.

Here is another example of a draw by repetition:

This position came out of the Pirc Defense. White just captured a queen but is not winning because Black has a hilarious sequence of moves beginning from this position, beginning with a check . . .

. . . moving the bishop from d4 to f2, defended by the knight on g4. Black's light-squared bishop on b5 cuts off two of the White king's escape options (the f1 and e2 squares), meaning White has only one move . . .

↑ . . . which is moving the king to d2. Black then plays another check . . .

↑ . . . moving the dark squared bishop to e3. White's king has only one option, returning to e1, at which point Black's bishop goes back to f2 and White is forced to repeat moves until it's a draw. There is nothing White can do—despite being down five points of material, Black forces a draw by repeating moves. This should give you a sense of when forcing a draw by repetition is useful.

Draw by Stalemate

The third method by which a game of chess can be drawn is by stalemate. We briefly touched on stalemate in Chapter Four when looking at the Queen and King Mate. Stalemate most often occurs in the endgame when an inexperienced player—or a player who hasn't done their checkmate practice—is trying to checkmate the opponent from a position where they have more material and should win. Stalemate is when a player has no legal moves but is *not* in check. Below is an example of a classic stalemate position:

↑ If it's Black to move here, it's a draw by stalemate. Black has no legal moves because all the immediate squares around the Black king are attacked by one of White's two pieces. Had Black's king been under a direct attack, this would be checkmate. But in this situation, Black is both not in check and cannot play a legal move (they'd have to move into check) so the game is drawn by stalemate—which is a heartbreaking way to draw a game of chess, especially here, where White is up a full queen! White should have used the King and Queen Mate technique we looked at in Chapter Four, keeping the queen in knight opposition to the enemy king and ensuring the king always has two squares to hop between before delivering mate.

Stalemate doesn't just happen in the corner of the board. Here is a more absurd example:

⬆ Here White is up not one queen but two queens! The Black king is completely out in the open but every single square surrounding it is attacked by one of the White queens. If it is Black's move, this is stalemate and a draw. How do you avoid stalemating your opponent here? White needed to coordinate their queens to deliver the Ladder Mate we looked at in Chapter Four.

Our final example is from one of my own games against my good friend and fellow International Master Eric Rosen:

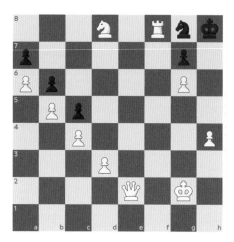

⬆ I was playing a blitz game (a game where each player begins with less than ten minutes on the clock) against Eric and captured his queen with my rook on f8. Under normal circumstances, capturing a queen for free is a great decision. But here—despite me being up 13 points of material—Eric has zero legal moves. In the previous examples the opponent only had a king on the board. In this example, my opponent has six pieces and *none* of them can move. All Black's pawns are blocked from moving forward, Black's knight is pinned to the Black king, and the Black king cannot move to h7 because that square is covered by my pawn on g6.

I have such a dominant position and am so close to delivering checkmate, but due to the fact that Eric does not have any legal moves, it's a draw by stalemate. What should I have done here instead? Instead of taking Eric's queen immediately, I should have ensured that every move would be a check. For example, moving my queen from e2 to h5 would check the Black king on h8. Then capturing his queen would have been checkmate. It happens to us all, especially in time scrambles!

Stalemate is something you need to be very wary of when you are up material in an endgame, because it results in a draw when you should win; likewise, if you are dead losing, look for any opportunities to trick your opponent into stalemating you with clumsy play. This means intentionally creating a situation where you have no legal moves, and hoping your opponent doesn't spot that it will be stalemate on your next move. It's worth pointing out that stalemates are incredibly rare at the highest level—grandmasters are too experienced and clever to blunder stalemate—but at lower levels it can and does happen.

50-Move Rule

A game is also drawn when each player plays 50 moves where no pieces are captured and no pawns are advanced. Similar to draw by repetition, this rule was implemented to prevent games going on forever. Of course, there is always a clock but in longer games players often get extra time per move they make (i.e., thirty seconds is added to your clock whenever you make a move, meaning games could theoretically continue forever!). Look at this position:

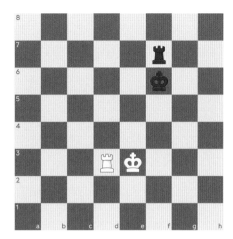

⬆ Here, one of the players should offer a draw by agreement and the other player should accept. But let's say both players are extremely stubborn. Let's say they hate each other and they plan on playing to the death, hoping that somehow their opponent will accidentally give away their rook. It's positions like this—and players like this—that make the 50-move rule necessary. Theoretically both players could play forever, shuffling their rooks around, playing checks without ever winning material.

Imagine if the Black rook were a knight in the example position. White would technically be up material—a rook is worth more than a knight—so White might want to play on. But rook versus knight is a theoretical draw, meaning if two computers or grandmasters played the position it would be a draw every time. Still, at the beginner and intermediate level, players might want to play this out, hoping Black might make a mistake and somehow lose their knight. If White plans on winning this endgame, this rule means White has 50 moves to do so.

Draw by Insufficient Checkmating Material

The final method of drawing a chess game is insufficient checkmating material, which we touched on briefly in Chapter One. What does this mean? Take the following position:

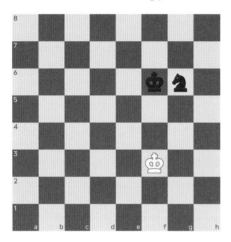

⬆ In this position the game ends on the spot and is declared a draw. There is no point of anybody playing this position. In this case, you're not even relying on a mistake from your opponent; it's impossible for either player to win or lose this position. Even though Black is up a knight, it's proven that you cannot checkmate an enemy king with only a king and a knight. There is no way to trap the enemy king in the corner and deliver mate with only a knight, so this is a draw by insufficient checkmating material. The same would be true if the Black knight were swapped for a bishop in this position.

A pawn, on the other hand (and despite being worth less than a knight or bishop), is not considered insufficient checkmating material:

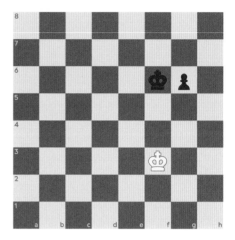

⬆ That's because a pawn can be promoted to a queen if Black can find a way to safely escort it to the bottom of the board.

Draw by insufficient checkmating material is another thing you need to keep in mind when playing endgames. Sometimes an opponent may look to sacrifice a knight or a bishop for your final pawn, for example, to force a draw. Likewise, this is another tool for you to draw upon if you're losing a game—if you have a king and a bishop and your opponent has a king, bishop, and pawn, if you capture the enemy pawn with your bishop it will be a draw by insufficient material.

To finish, I want to show you a special example of a draw by insufficient material. We've talked before about time controls in chess. Well, imagine one player is completely winning and has a massive material advantage, as in this position:

⬆ Let's say White has just moved their king to d1 and before Black can play their next move, their clock runs out. Ordinarily, losing on time means losing, even if you have a big advantage. But in cases like this position, even though Black has run out of time, the game is a draw because White does not have sufficient material to ever checkmate Black.

So even though White might expect to win when Black's clock hits zero, the result here is a draw. If White had any other pieces in this position—even a pawn—White would win when Black's clock runs out, even though Black has a massive advantage. This position is actually another one of mine from an online blitz game. I'm playing with the Black pieces here and I'm about to deliver checkmate; in fact, I have four different checkmates here (try to find them).* But I lost on time in this position, meaning my clock ran out before I could drag my queen to checkmate White. So, the game ended in a draw—and it hurt.

---

* Moving the queen to any of d2, f1, g1, or h1 would all have been checkmate!

Summary

Now you know all the different ways that games of chess can be drawn: by agreement, repetition, stalemate, the 50-move rule, and insufficient checkmating material. You understand why in some situations you should try to make a draw (e.g., from a worse or totally lost position), and we've looked at some of the tricks and tools at your disposal to try to salvage that draw. On the other hand, be wary of your opponents looking to rescue draws from positions where you are winning. Given the various ways draws can be achieved in chess, my advice to beginners is always the same: never resign. Play the game out to its conclusion because you never know when your opponent will accidentally stalemate you, be forced to repeat moves, or run out of time.

Follow this QR code to explore some of the draw scenarios covered in this chapter.

CHAPTER SEVEN

ATTACKING, DEFENDING, AND CAPTURING

So far we've looked at the basics of the opening and some straightforward checkmating and endgame scenarios. But how does a game of chess transform from the opening—with thirty-two pieces on the board—to some of the endgame situations we've looked at? In this chapter, we'll be delving deeper into the **middlegame**, particularly how pieces "see" the board, see other pieces (both your own and your opponent's), and interact with one another. This will then lead into a discussion on **tactics**—move combinations you need to look for in a game of chess that result in winning material.

Piece Vision

Let's begin by looking at what I mean by pieces "seeing" the board. Every chess piece can see. The squares each piece can see means the squares (occupied or not) they could move to from their current position. Any given piece will be able to see any of three things from whichever square they currently

occupy: their own pieces, empty squares, or enemy pieces. Let's look at a queen on an empty board:

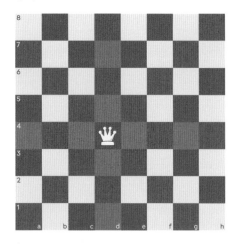

♟ Highlighted in red are all the squares the queen can see on a central square of an empty board. That's twenty-seven squares—nearly half the entire board. That shows the power of the queen.

Every piece sees the most from the center of the board, which goes back to what we learned in the openings chapters. Let's swap the queen with a knight:

⬆ From this central square, the knight sees eight different squares. We call this an Octopus Knight, which is a knight at its most powerful. A knight in the very corner of the board would only see two squares and would be much less effective.

You can see here that the other major pieces, the rook and the bishop, have the widest vision of the board from the center, too (actually a rook can see 14 squares from wherever it's positioned, which is one reason it's worth more than bishops and knights):

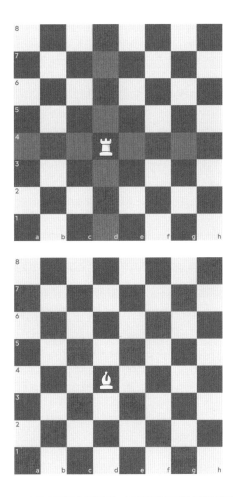

♚ **FUN FACT**

If you tally up how many squares the rook and bishop see from the d4 square, their combined total is 27—the same as the queen on its own!

Clearly you won't find yourself in situations where there is only a single piece on the board, so let's incorporate some other pieces:

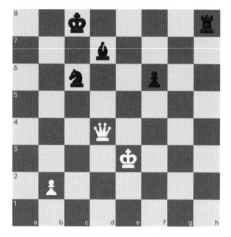

⬆ Let's now build on what pieces see by bringing in some terms we've touched upon before: **attacking**, **defending**, and **capturing**. White's queen is on the same spot it was when it was alone on the board, the d4 square. But now the board is busier.

From this position, which pieces does the White queen see? You might have said the Black pawn and bishop, which is partially correct, but it's just as important to think about *which of your own pieces* your other pieces can see:

⬆ The White queen could capture either the Black bishop or Black pawn. Likewise, the queen **defends** the White pawn, meaning if a Black piece were to capture it, the White queen would then be able to capture that piece. The White queen does not see the Black rook on h8 even though they are on the same diagonal, because Black's pawn is in the way—something we call **blocking**.

To bring back our terms, in this position we say the queen is **attacking** Black's pawn on f6. We say attacking because none of the other Black pieces are defending that pawn, so if it's White's turn in this position the White queen can capture it for free. The White queen can also see the bishop and technically can capture it; however, it isn't attacking the bishop because the bishop is defended by Black's king (meaning that if the White queen captured that bishop, the Black king could then recapture the White queen).

Now let's look at the next position but include all the squares (not just the pieces) that the queen can see:

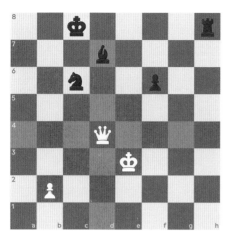

⬆ On this slightly busier board, the queen sees 21 squares but only has 19 moves. The queen cannot move to the squares occupied by the White king and pawn. You can see how the enemy pieces—or your own pieces—can block the vision of your pieces.

Let's again look at this position but now from Black's perspective. In red are the squares all Black's pieces can see:

✏ Black poses a very clear threat, which is that Black's knight is attacking the White queen. While we know that it isn't *necessarily* an attack if the piece is defended, this is very much an attack. That's because the queen is worth so much more than a knight. So even though the White king would immediately capture the Black knight, a queen for a knight would be a very bad trade for White and a very good trade for Black.

So, in this position, White should move the queen to prevent it being captured by Black. The best move is probably to capture the Black pawn on f6—which both gets the queen to safety and wins material for White.

This is how the concepts of vision, attacking, and defending combine in any given position in chess. Each of your pieces sees a combination of empty squares, enemy pieces, and your own pieces. You want your pieces to be seeing as many squares as possible: attacking as many enemy pieces as possible, defending as many of your own pieces as possible, and seeing lots of empty squares, which gives your pieces flexibility in terms of moving and also can prevent enemy pieces from occupying those empty squares.

Attacking and Defending

Let's look at some more examples regarding the dynamics involved in attacking and defending. Take this position:

🡑 Here there are no obvious moves for White. There are no captures. There are no checks or checkmates. So, what should you do if you're playing White? Well, you can attack Black's queen. How would you do it?

By moving the knight to f4, the White knight now sees the Black queen and attacks it. You might have noticed that moving the knight to c5 would also attack the Black queen, but remember that the Black bishop sees that square and would immediately capture your knight. 🖋

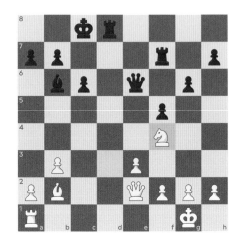

In this position, our knight is threatening to capture the Black queen. Given that the queen is the most valuable piece, Black should move the queen. Moving is one way to defend a piece that is under attack, but not the only way. We touched on another way to defend in chess in the above example. Let's say you did attack the Black queen by moving your knight to c5:

✎ Here Black could absolutely still defend their queen by moving it. But Black has a better defense here, which is capturing the White knight with their bishop.

📍 So, we see here how moving a piece under attack is one kind of defense, and capturing the attacking piece is a second kind of defense. Let's look at another example:

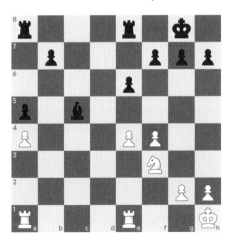

✎ Here a good move for White would be to attack Black's bishop with one of our rooks. This simultaneously threatens to capture material while also developing one of our rooks to a more active position. Technically either of White's rooks can move to the square that achieves this, but let's say in this position we move our a rook from a1 to c1.

📍 This creates an attack on the Black bishop. Now the bishop could absolutely move out the way of our attack. But for instructional purposes let's say Black chooses a different way to defend the bishop. If it's a higher-value piece attacking a lower-value piece (a rook is worth more than a bishop), Black can simply defend the bishop ...

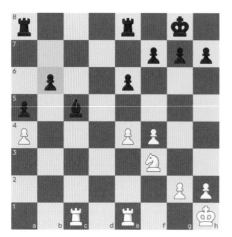

♟ . . . by pushing their pawn from b7 to b6. Now if White's rook captures the Black bishop, the pawn will recapture the rook. White will have lost five points of material and Black will have lost three—it's a bad trade for White! Black could also protect the bishop with one of their rooks . . .

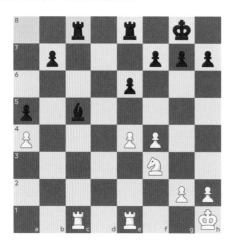

♟ . . . this is the third way of defending against an attack: bringing another piece to protect it.

The fourth and final way of defending against an attack on one of your pieces is blocking the attack. This often happens with checks but can happen with attacks on any of your pieces. Look at this position:

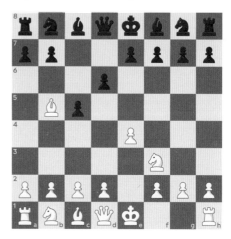

♟ This is from the Sicilian Defense and only the third move of the game. Black's king is under attack from White's bishop—it is in check. Here Black cannot move the king (and shouldn't even if they could), cannot capture the White bishop, and obviously cannot protect the king from being captured with another piece. So, the only defensive resource left for Black is to block the attack. That means putting another of their pieces between the bishop and the king so the king is no longer under attack.

Black has four different options for blocking the attack. One of them would be moving the queen to d7, which would be catastrophically bad since the White bishop will capture the queen and Black will have given up their most valuable piece. So Black should either move the knight (the knight can block on either c6 or d7) or the bishop into the path between White's bishop and the Black king:

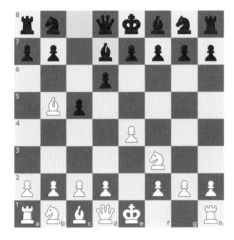

⬆ Let's say Black moves their bishop to d7. A bishop for a bishop would be an even trade, and if White captures Black's bishop, Black can recapture with either their knight or queen. This is the most forcing move because not only has Black defended their king, but Black now attacks White's bishop with their own bishop. So White has to do something about that, either by capturing Black's bishop or moving their own bishop away.

Let's look at another example of blocking:

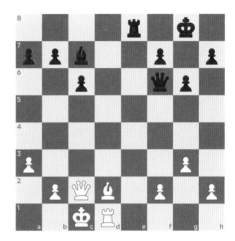

⬆ Let's say that in this position White would like to attack Black's queen.

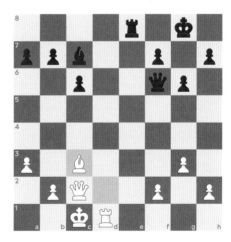

⬆ To do so, White plays bishop to c3. This attacks Black's queen. Black cannot capture the bishop with their queen because this would be a horrible trade—capturing the bishop with the queen would mean Black losing their queen in the next turn. Black *could* protect the queen with either their bishop, rook, or king, but again this would result in a losing trade for Black because White's bishop would capture Black's queen and Black would only capture the bishop in return. Black could move the queen to protect it, but instead let's say Black chooses a blocking move . . .

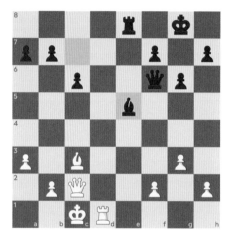

⬆ . . . by playing bishop to e5. Black's bishop intervenes between White's bishop and the Black queen. Again this is quite a forcing move because Black has blocked with a piece that attacks in return, but other pieces can also block—even if they can't attack in return, they are there to protect a higher-value piece.

So, there are a lot of ways to defend in chess: moving, protecting, capturing the attacking piece, and blocking. As you play more chess, you'll learn more about which type of defense to draw upon in situations where you have a choice. Moving the threatened piece is a good choice when you can move it to a more advantageous square,

either by capturing a loose enemy piece or creating a new threat yourself. Capturing the attacking piece makes sense in any situation where the trade will be even or better for you (i.e., you are trading off pieces of equal value or even trading one of your lesser pieces for a better opposing piece). Protecting the attacked piece is useful in scenarios where you are both defending the piece and improving the position of the piece you use to defend it. And finally, blocking is at its most effective when you are blocking with a piece that also likewise attacks.

I also want to point out the difference between seeing a piece and attacking it:

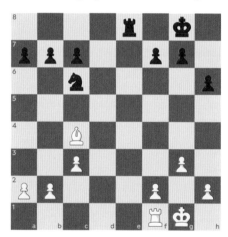

⬆ In this position, the White bishop sees the Black pawn on f7. But it's not an attack because you're not threatening to take it. You have eyes on it but if you took it, you would simply lose your bishop for a pawn—a bad trade—when the Black king recaptures your bishop.

Last but not least, I want to cover another example of something that's not an attack in chess, even though it looks like one. When I used to teach beginners, this was something they regularly struggled to understand. In the same position, if playing White, my former students would usually play something like rook to e1:

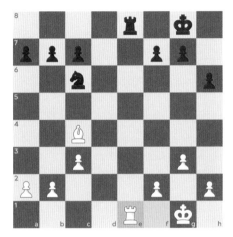

⬆ Looks like an attack, right? We're threatening to take the Black rook with our own rook. In explaining why they chose this move, beginners would often say things like "maybe they won't notice the threat." That is not how I'm trying to teach you to play chess. Never play a move on the basis of hoping your opponent won't notice something. The key here is that you cannot attack a piece with the same piece, that is, you cannot attack a rook with a rook, because the opposing rook attacks your rook right back. They see each other, and it's your opponent's turn . . .

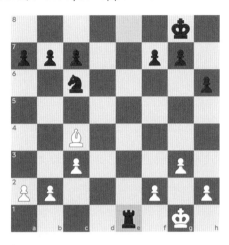

⬆ . . . and so here you simply lose a rook for nothing.

Tactics

Tactics in chess are forcing sequences or combinations—combining everything we've looked at about attacking and defending—that result in material gain. Some tactics result in winning an opposing piece or two for free; others result in you winning more valuable pieces in exchange for one of your own less valuable pieces (like trading a bishop for an enemy rook, or your pawn for an enemy knight). Tactics are really the key to getting from the opening to a winning endgame.

If both players make even trades through-out every stage of the game, the game will end in a draw with two kings on the board and nothing else.

Forks

The easiest and most fun tactic to learn is the **fork**. A fork is a tactic in chess where your single piece simultaneously attacks two or more opposing pieces. If you can do this successfully, the opponent will not be able to defend both pieces at the same time and you'll be guaranteed to win material. Take this position:

⬆ From this position, where could you move the White queen so that it attacks two pieces at the same time?

⬆ If you said queen to a4 (which is check), you are correct. From a4, the queen simulta-neously attacks the Black king and the Black bishop. However Black defends against the check, the White queen will capture the Black bishop on their next turn and be up material. Note that the White queen is not only seeing the Black king and bishop, but also the pawn on a7. However, that pawn is defended by the Black rook so isn't a real attack.

This is a fork. They often happen with a check—where the opponent is forced to pro-tect their king—but can happen in other situations, too. Forks most commonly involve knights. The knight is especially dangerous at forking opposing pieces because no other pieces move like a knight. This means that when a knight attacks a pawn, bishop, rook, queen, or king, that piece can't also be attack-ing the knight in return—whereas, for example, rooks and queens attack each other, or pawns attack each other, etc. Look at this position:

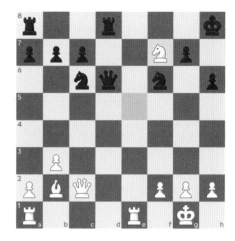

♟ It's White's turn to move and play a devastating fork that practically wins the game. Look at the next board.

The White knight jumps to f7, capturing the pawn but also delivering what's known as a "family fork"—it simultaneously attacks Black's rook, queen, and king—the full set. None of Black's pieces can capture the knight so Black has to move their king out of check, at which point the knight will promptly capture the Black queen and gain a huge material advantage. ✎

Forks in chess are extremely fun, not to mention powerful. At the end of this chapter, follow the QR code to practice some forks.

Before we move on, let's look at something that is still a fork but doesn't necessarily win any material:

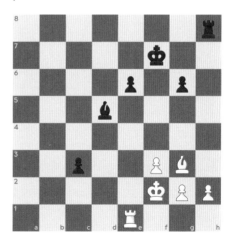

♟ In this position, White can play a move that attacks two pieces at the same time. Can you find it?

⬇ White can play bishop to e5, simultaneously attacking Black's rook in the corner and the pawn on c3. That's a fork, right? Technically, yes. But Black can move one of the pieces under attack to defend the other one . . .

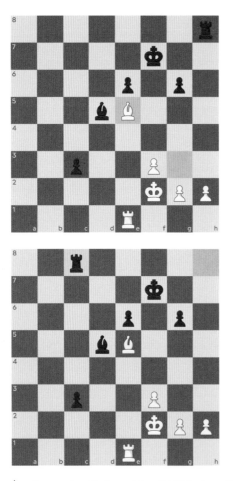

⬆ . . . by moving their rook to c8. White hasn't lost any material here, but the Black rook is now arguably in a better position, supporting

the pawn as it marches toward promotion. It's worth bearing this in mind for any move you play in chess, whether attempting a fork or just a straightforward attack: ask yourself where the opponent is going to move the attacked piece. Oftentimes beginners overlook where the attacked piece will move and end up in more trouble than they've created for the opponent.

A more egregious example of when a fork isn't really a fork is this position:

⬆ The White queen technically sees four of Black's pieces in this position: the knight and the pawns on b7, d6, and f7. So technically it's a four-way fork. But the queen shouldn't take any of these pieces because they're all protected—it would simply mean giving up a queen for a lesser piece. This is not a situation where the queen is legitimately threatening to win any material. Ask yourself when trying to fork pieces: If those pieces are defended, will I actually be winning any material?

Pins

The next tactic we're going to look at is something called a pin. Pins are very simple but can be very powerful. A pin is when a particular piece cannot move because it would expose a more valuable piece behind it to being captured. This typically happens when a knight or bishop is pinned to a queen, rook, or king, but can occur with other combinations of pieces. Let's start with this position:

⬆ Here the Black bishop on g4 is pinning the White knight to the White queen. If the White knight were to move, the bishop would capture the White queen and Black would be winning material. This is known as a **relative pin**: a relative pin is when a player can legally move the pinned piece but would be losing material by doing so.

That's different from an **absolute pin**, where it's illegal to move the pinned piece because it stands between the attacker and the king:

⬆ This is an absolute pin. Black's bishop on b4 pins the knight on c3 to White's king. The knight cannot move because it would be check. If you are playing this game online, the software won't let you move the knight. If you're playing over-the-board, hopefully you or your opponent will spot it if an illegal move is played; otherwise the game will end up being voided.

So, in a relative pin you can theoretically move, though it would be a horrible move if it meant losing a higher-value piece. With an absolute pin you legally cannot move the pinned piece, so have to get rid of the attacking piece or move the king out of the pin. Both types of pins are powerful because they restrict an opposing piece from moving and can lead to you capturing pieces for free if the opponent isn't able to get themselves out of the pin or defend the pinned piece in time. This ties into a concept known as "putting pressure on the pinned piece." Look at this position:

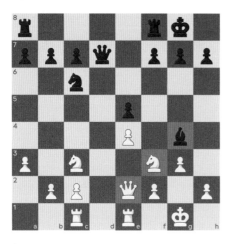

⬆ Black's bishop has pinned White's knight on f3 to the White queen. Black could capture the knight, but it's defended by the queen and would be an even trade. Instead, Black should increase the pressure on the pinned piece by playing knight to d4.

➡ This is a devastating position for White. White cannot capture the Black knight with their own knight because the Black bishop would then see the queen and capture it; likewise the Black knight is directly attacking the White queen. White's only option is to move the queen to safety, at which point Black will capture the White knight on f3 (with either their knight or bishop) and be up material.

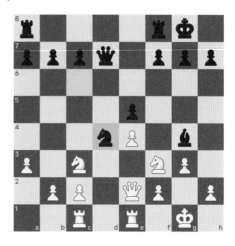

This should give you a sense of how potent pins can be from an attacking viewpoint, as well as highlight how it's important not to stay in pinned positions from a defensive stance. Pressure can quickly be added to the pinned piece, which can result in losing material. It's worth thinking about this when you draw on one of the defensive resources we talked about earlier, blocking the attack. Blocking can be effective, but it can also lead to positions where you have pinned yourself, so try to think about this before rushing to block an attack with one of your pieces.

We've looked only at bishops pinning but other pieces can pin, too, as shown in this example:

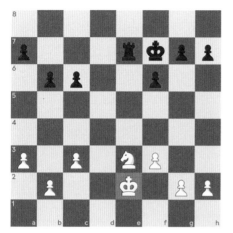

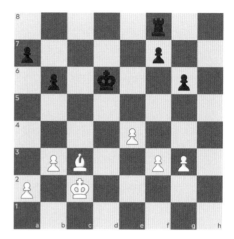

↑ Here the Black rook pins the White knight to the White king. Likewise, you could replace the rook with a queen in this position and it would still be a pin. Right now, the pin isn't achieving much except restricting the movement of the White knight, but if White doesn't act then Black could march their f pawn down the board and threaten to capture the White knight if White hasn't found a way to unpin themselves before then.

Skewers

The next tactic you should be aware of is a **skewer**. A skewer is essentially an inverse pin: you create an attack on a higher-value piece that, when moved, allows you to capture another piece behind it. Skewers most often feature kings:

↑ In this endgame, Black was doing pretty well but has left their king and rook on the same diagonal—overlooking a tactic for White, which is bishop to b4.

This is check and now Black's king is skewered by the White bishop. Wherever Black moves the king, the bishop will take the rook behind it and win a valuable piece. Black has suddenly gone from probably winning to probably losing. ◄

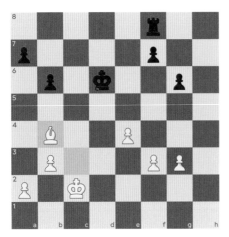

Here is another example of a skewer:

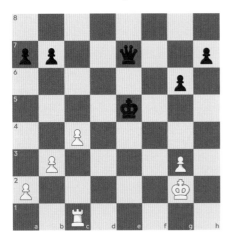

⬆ In this example, Black is winning—Black has a queen and White has a rook. But Black has left their king and queen on the same file, so White plays rook to e1, skewering the Black king and winning the Black queen behind it.

In this scenario, what is the best move for Black? We know that Black has to move the king and so is certainly going to lose the queen, but *where* should Black move the king? Black needs to move to either d6 or f6, so that when White's rook captures the queen, Black can recapture the rook with the king. If Black moves the king anywhere else, they lose the queen for nothing! ⬇

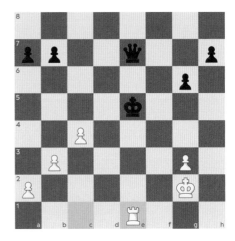

This should give you a feel for how powerful skewers are. They typically involve an attack on the king but it could also be that you attack a queen, rook, or any piece that is forced to move, allowing you to capture a lesser piece behind it.

Discovered Attacks

Finally, another really important tactic to know is the **discovered attack**. Everything in this chapter has led up to this concept. To really improve your chess, you need to be able to see how the board changes whenever a piece is moved. In the case of discovered attacks, it's crucial that you can visualize what pieces will suddenly be able to see when a piece that was previously blocking their vision is moved out the way. We touched on this with pins—in a relative pin, moving the pinned piece out of the way will result in you losing material. Discovered attacks are an offensive tactic where you deliberately move one of your own pieces to create an attack from one of your own pieces behind it.

Let's take this position:

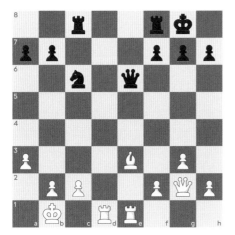

⬆ If I asked you in this position how you could attack Black's rook on f8, what would you play?

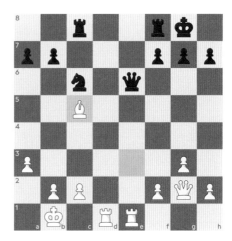

⬆ Based on everything you've learned in this chapter, hopefully you found the answer, which is bishop to c5. But look what else has happened by moving your bishop. Ordinarily Black would move the rook out of danger but White has two attacks in this position: the bishop attacking the rook on f8 but *also* the rook on e1 now attacking the Black queen.

So, White's rook is creating a discovered attack, and White threatens two problems at once. A queen is worth more than a rook, so Black should choose to move the queen to safety, at which the White bishop will capture the rook on f8 and White will be up material. Bear in mind that this only works in this position because White's rook on e1 is protected by the other rook—otherwise the Black queen would be able to capture it.

Discovered Checks

One of the most powerful tactics in chess is a form of discovered attack called the **discovered check**. A discovered check follows the same principle as a discovered attack—moving one piece out of the way to reveal an attack from a different piece—except the revealed attack is now also a check on the enemy king. Take this position:

⬆ Here Black's king in the corner can be attacked by White's bishop on b2. But White's knight is in the way. Wherever White moves the knight, it will be check. The White knight has five possible moves but two of them are devastating for Black . . .

If the knight moves to either of the squares highlighted here, b5 or e6, White's knight will threaten Black's queen, and there is nothing Black can do. Black has to move their king out of check, meaning on White's next turn they'll be able to capture the Black queen for free. This is what makes discovered checks so devastating—always look for opportunities to set up attacks of these kinds, as well as making sure your own king isn't in danger of discovered checks. ⬇

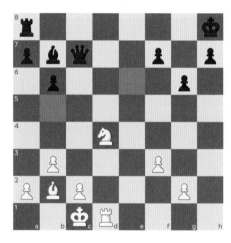

Summary

Understanding how all the pieces interact on a chessboard is foundational to your future chess endeavors. Once you understand the dynamics of attack and defense, you can begin practicing more forcing patterns known as tactics.

- Vision refers to the line of sight for any given piece. Pieces usually all see a combination of three things: the enemy, the same side, and empty squares.
- When you attack a piece, you create a tangible threat of material gain. Attacking moves do not signify good moves, but merely showcase your understanding of piece interactions. Remember: seeing a piece is not the same as attacking it.
- In some cases, the defending piece cannot even see the threat coming (think of a knight attacking a queen). However, if you attacked a queen with your bishop, they would see each other—so the bishop would need some defense, or else the queen would capture. Be careful when creating attacks between pieces with similar abilities.
- Defense, in turn, is the opposite of attack. Pieces can protect each other from captures due to the hierarchy of point values. Defense can also refer to the avoidance of danger—moving out of the way or blocking against an enemy assault.

In this chapter we also dove into tactics, which feature short, forced combinations for immediate gain.

- Forks are situations where one piece attacks multiple enemy targets, guaranteeing some form of return. At the least, you may win a pawn; at the most, you deliver checkmate.
- Pins occur when a piece of lower value stands on the same diagonal or straightaway as one of higher value. It is important to remember that moving the weaker piece will result in the loss of the more valuable one behind it. When pinning a piece, you should apply more pressure on it.
- Skewers are the inverse of pins—first, you create a threat on a stronger piece, necessitating a response, and then winning the second piece after the initial threat.
- In discovered attacks, one piece moves and opens up an attack created by the previously covered one. In a perfect situation, both pieces will create threats of their own, resulting in a devastating situation for your opponent.

 Follow this QR code to practice some of the tactics covered in this chapter.

CHAPTER EIGHT
BEGINNER STRATEGY

Chapter Seven was pretty intense but hopefully you've come through with a firmer grasp on how pieces can interact and combine in a tactical way. This chapter will look at the other side of chess, which is strategy. Tactics and strategy are quite different but both are important. As we saw in the last chapter, tactics are short-term combinations of moves that result in quick material gain. Strategy, on the other hand, is looking long term and doesn't necessarily involve immediate material gain. An example of strategy might be making the decision to focus your attack on the enemy kingside, where you envision strong long-term prospects of breaking through with pawns or boxing in the enemy king.

Learning strategy is important because it helps you better understand how to evaluate a position and—based on the placement of the pieces—start to develop long-term plans that leave you in a winning endgame. Tactical situations are similar but there is always that quick win or gain. In strategy or positional play, you can learn to read the board and determine who is better or worse in positions where material is equal. Let's take a look at some of the areas that feed into strategic thinking.

Weaknesses

A weakness can mean a piece, a square, or an area of the board that is inadequately defended and therefore is exploitable for either immediate or long-term gain. I know I said strategy is more about the long term but sometimes a weakness can offer both short-term prospects and long-term advantage, depending on how your opponent responds to your threats.

Let's start with this position:

✏ If you examine the board and count the material, you'll see it's completely equal. But material is not the entire story and that's what this chapter is going to teach you. If you look closely at this position, one of Black's pieces is not protected by anything. Can you spot which one?

It's a little bit of a trick question because actually Black's rook in the corner on h8 is also not protected by any other Black piece but it's impossible to attack right now. Instead, we should focus on Black's knight on c6, which isn't defended by any of Black's pieces—remember, pawns only capture diagonally, so none of the pawns surrounding the knight protect it. Because it's not defended, we should attack it and try to win some material. Based on what we learned in the last chapter, how can we put pressure on this knight? There are actually two ways to pin the knight to the Black king but for sake of ease let's pin the knight with our bishop by moving our bishop to b5:

✏ Now the knight is both attacked and pinned, Black's only way to defend the knight is to move their king toward the knight to protect it with the king itself . . .

⬆ As you might remember from the Introduction, once you move your king anywhere you are no longer able to castle, so this is bad for Black. And White can make it even worse. Can you see a way to add even more pressure to Black's weakness? We put pressure on the pinned piece . . .

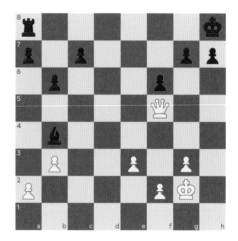

♙ . . . by moving our queen to a4. Black is going to lose their knight. They cannot move it because doing so would expose their king (an illegal move) and cannot bring in any other pieces to bolster its defense. White will now be able to capture the Black knight with their bishop on the next move, and Black's king won't be able to recapture the bishop because White's queen defends it.

This is a very simple introduction to spotting weakness. In any position, it's always worth having a scan for any pieces in your opponent's position that aren't protected and looking for ways to exploit that. Here's another example:

♙ Here you should be able to spot that a couple of Black's pieces are not protected and—as luck would have it—White has a queen, the most powerful attacker in all of chess. White has several options to attack either Black's rook or Black's bishop with the queen. But White also has a way to attack *both* at the same time—a fork—which is playing queen to e4.

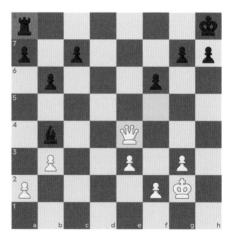

✒ White's queen now attacks both Black's rook on a8 and their bishop on b4 and it's impossible for Black to save them both. Black should of course save the rook; first because a rook is worth more, but second because in this particular position it would be Back-Rank Mate if White's queen captures Black's rook!

All we did here was look around and ask what pieces in Black's position are weak, meaning undefended. It may seem like we are covering the same tactics from the last chapter, but we are finding these tactics with strategic thinking, looking for weaknesses, and coming up with ideas to exploit them. That's how strategy and tactics intersect.

It's important to note that a weakness isn't always so obvious, as in this third example:

♟ Here we're in an endgame. Almost everything has been traded and if you compare the material, White is only up one pawn, which on its own isn't substantial enough to secure victory. But if you study the position more closely, you'll notice that Black's two pawns on the b7 and c6 could be weaknesses, and White has a way to attack them both at the same time . . .

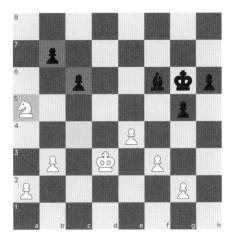

♟ . . . by playing knight to a5. This guarantees White will win at least one pawn. Right now, the knight attacks the b7 pawn and, if Black moves it forward, the c6 pawn is suddenly undefended and the White knight can capture that one instead. Either way, White will be up two pawns in an endgame instead of one, which is a much more decisive advantage.

So, a weakness doesn't always have to be super obvious or compelling—look for any pieces that are undefended, not just hanging queens (although, if you see your opponent has left their queen unguarded, please do take it). It can be as simple as winning a pawn in an endgame.

For the next two examples, I want to look at situations where certain squares—rather than pieces—are weak. Look at this position, for example:

⬆ Here Black is actually up three points of material. Black has an extra knight. But you might be surprised to learn that White can win from this position in three moves— meaning if White finds the correct three moves, there's nothing Black can do to avoid being mated. This is because there are certain squares around the Black king that are weak. Two considerations go into whether or not a square or squares are weak. First, as with pieces, are the squares in question protected or not? Second, are the majority of the nearby enemy pawns on the opposite color of the square you're evaluating?

That might seem a little complicated, but the previous position should help illustrate it better. The f6 and h6 squares are not defended by any of Black's pieces, meaning White could put a piece on either square. Similarly, the g7 square is only defended by the Black king, so if two of White's pieces attacked this square at the same time Black would be in trouble. Notice how all of Black's pawns nearest the Black king are on light squares. Remember that pawns capture diagonally, meaning pawns only protect squares of the same color as the square they occupy. So, all of Black's pawns surrounding the king have left the dark squares up for grabs—the pawns near the king can't capture any White pieces that land on those dark squares. Black's position is like Swiss cheese—full of holes.

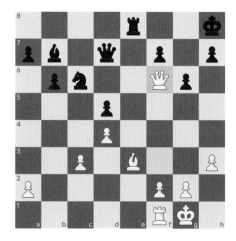

⬆ In this position White has two pieces that are fully equipped to exploit Black's dark-squared weaknesses: the queen and the bishop. So in this position White would play queen to f6, which is check. In response, black has only one move . . .

... which is moving the king to g8. ↓

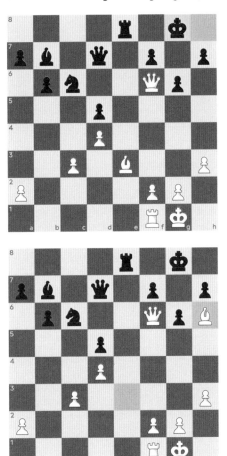

↑ Next, White brings the bishop to h6. Because of Black's dark-squared weaknesses, there is no way for Black to prevent queen to g7 checkmate on White's next move. Black is up material and has strong pieces on the board but because of the weaknesses around their king, they lose the game.

Here's an example looking at light-squared weaknesses instead of dark-squared weaknesses.

↑ Black has three pawns on dark squares, which means the light squares surrounding the Black king are vulnerable.

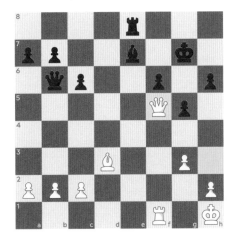

↑ White should begin their attack with queen to f5. The queen and the bishop are now lined up on the same diagonal and are about to break into the king's house. It's going to be bad news and Black is going to lose in a few moves. White will use checks to bully the Black king into the corner, either delivering checkmate or else winning some Black pieces.

This is how squares can be weak and can be exploited, either by yourself or your opponent. Just to illustrate how dangerous it can be to have all your pawns on the same-color square around your king, look at the below position:

⬆ This position is practically identical to the previous example, except one pawn changed position in the Black defense—the h6 pawn is now a g6 pawn. This position is completely equal, meaning with best play this would likely end in a draw. White is no longer in a much stronger position because the light squares around the Black king are no longer free for White's pieces to laser through. The defense of the Black king is stronger due to that one small change.

Having pawns—particularly those surrounding your king—on a good balance of light and dark squares gives you much better protection. We'll talk more about pawns later, but for now it's important to see how badly organized pawns can create weakness in your defense. Knowing how to position and structure your pawns is a big part of chess—after all, you have more pawns than any other piece so it pays to know how to use them.

Space

Space in chess is not the most straightforward concept. In the simplest terms, space means the number of squares you control in your opponent's territory (i.e., the opposing four ranks of the board). By "control," I mean a square on which one of your pieces could capture an enemy piece if it appeared. Let's look at an example position.

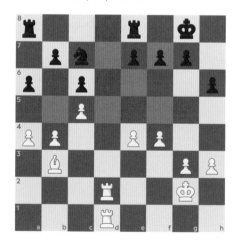

✎ Highlighted are all the squares in Black territory that White controls. Theoretically, if Black put a piece on any of these squares, White could capture it. Whether White should capture it depends on the piece and whether it would be a good trade or not, but that's not the point. The point is that White controls ten squares in Black's territory and so we say White has much more space than Black in this position.

Now look at how many squares Black controls in the White position. How many? That's right—zero! So White is doing very well in this position. When you have a massive space advantage, you constrict your opponent's movement and give your own pieces lots of flexibility in their moves and lots of space to move into. Space is very important in chess and as you improve at the game you'll realize how much easier it is when you take as much space as possible on the board, and leave as little as possible for your opponent.

Of course, it's worth noting that space is not permanent. Like everything in chess, it constantly changes as moves are made and it's constantly being fought over. If you find yourself in a position where you lack space, trading pieces can be an effective way to change the balance in your favor. Trading off an opposing piece or pawn that controls squares in your territory takes space from your opponent and could swing the space war in your favor.

Think back to what we learned about the opening, particularly the golden moves (pages 26–28). Look at this position:

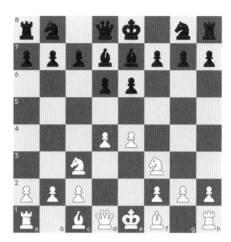

⬆ Here White has developed normally. White has followed the golden moves. Black has developed like a bozo, playing two timid pawn moves—moving them one square forward instead of two—and restricting the movement of their own bishops. Here, after just four moves, White controls eight squares in Black territory, while Black controls just two in White's territory.

Clearly that doesn't mean it's game over—there is still much chess to be played—but White has made a much better start and Black is going to struggle to make any progress if White keeps developing logically. Losing space from the opening can mean you spend much of the game trying to win it back, with your pieces suffocated by your opponent's and your movement restricted.

Let's look at another position out of the opening:

⬆ This came out of the Sicilian Defense, one of the most popular openings at the higher level of chess. If you count up the squares each side controls in the opposing territory, it's very even, with White controlling 14 and Black controlling 15. This is a much more balanced position where both sides are competing for the space on the board.

Let's look at one more example:

⬆ This is a position from the Scotch Opening. Both sides have made nine moves and White just edges the number of squares controlled in the opponent's territory, controlling 12 to Black's 10. But it's close and that is the way chess should be played, with both sides taking as much space as possible without putting their pieces in danger of being captured for free.

So what should you do if you lack space? Let's look a little closer at fighting back when suffering from a lack of space:

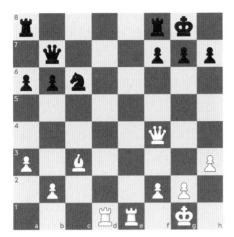 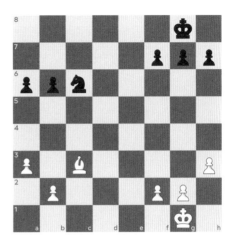

⬆ If you look at the material here, it's completely equal—both sides have 27 points of material. However, White is completely winning here and again it's because of space. Between White's pieces they control 14 empty squares in the Black half of the board. Black controls 2. White is not winning *because* of space—the score isn't 14-2 or something like that—but rather White's space advantage could lead to a powerful attack and material gain.

But let's look at how that can change if certain pieces are traded:

⬆ Here we have the same position, except let's imagine that all the rooks and queens have been traded. The position is now completely equal and could very well end in a draw. White now controls 3 squares in Black's territory and Black still controls just 2. White lost their space advantage by trading off the pieces. The lesson here is not to rush to trade pieces if you are dominating in terms of space. A rook for a rook is worth the same number of points, but a rook that controls lots of squares is worth a lot more than a rook that doesn't!

Conversely, when you are lacking space, you should be looking to trade enemy pieces that control lots of space in your territory to tip the balance in your favor. The same applies for pawns—trading off thorny opposing pawns in your position with less powerful pawns of your own can be a very effective way to get back into the game.

Closed vs. Open Positions

Positions in chess are determined to be either closed or open based on one and only one factor: Where are all the pawns? Think of pawns like a fence. Each player starts with a perfect fence of eight pawns on the 2nd or 7th ranks. If something like this happens:

♟ You might be able to guess just by looking that this is a closed position, which means very few pawns have been traded and the pawns are mostly frozen in place by the opposing pawns. (By the way, if this position ever happens in a real game you play, you and your opponent both need chess therapy.) This is the most closed a chess position can possibly be, with the two fences pressed up against each other, preventing either side from ever breaking through.

Now let's look at a very different position:

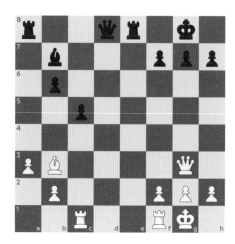

♟ Here the sides have traded three pawns each and a bunch of pieces. This is a very open position. Pieces can see from one side of the board to the other with little or no obstruction from pawns. The White queen can see a long diagonal. Black's queen and rook see the length of the board, as does Black's bishop on b7. These kinds of positions can be tricky for beginners who forget that the board is big—in open positions, pieces can still capture from the far side of the board if there's nothing in their way!

That should give you a sense of open versus closed positions. In closed positions, there tends to be blockades of pawns that shut off diagonal, vertical, and horizontal movement of the major pieces. In open positions, the pawn fences have fallen or are full of holes. Oftentimes the more open a position is, the more hectic it is, with pieces seeing each other from all sides of the boards. Neither a closed nor an open position is inherently better than the other. You just need to be able to recognize them and appreciate whether making a position open or closed is to your or your opponent's advantage, as well as understanding how to play them both. For example, an open position—where the pawn fence is full of holes—suits long-range pieces like bishops. If your opponent has two bishops and you have none, you might want to keep your position closed. And vice versa—if you have bishops and your opponent doesn't, an open position will provide open lines for your bishops to travel across the board.

Beginners can often struggle with closed positions when it seems there is no obvious way through. Drawing upon the principles we covered regarding space should help you in closed positions. You need to find trade opportunities—either pawns or other pieces that you can trade off with your opponent's pawns or pieces—that undermine the opponent's blockade, or else give you space, open lines, or pieces positioned on better squares, to help you break through the closed position.

Whether a position ends up open or closed depends on how the players want to play the game. Certain openings are more likely to create open or closed positions, for example the French Defense, Advance Variation:

⬆ White has only played three moves and Black only two. White has a strong pawn on e5, protected by their pawn on d4. Think about the concept of space that we've discussed in this chapter. White's e5 pawn is wedged in Black's position and prevents Black from putting a piece on either the d6 or f6 squares. So, a move that Black often relies upon in the French Defense . . .

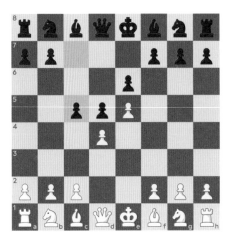

♟ . . . is moving a pawn to c5. Black is trying to undermine the defense of the e5 pawn as well as take space on the queenside. If Black captures the d4 pawn, or if White captures Black's c5 pawn, the White pawn on e5 becomes a lot weaker since it is no longer defended. This is the kind of thing you can use when trying to break through closed positions: pushing pawns to attack and undermine the enemy pawn structure.

Another example of a closed position is the very famous King's Indian Defense:

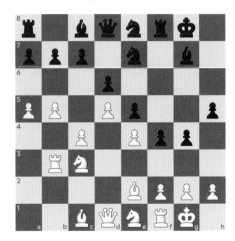

♙ Garry Kasparov, one of the greatest players of all time, used this defense a lot. Here's a typical position in the King's Indian Defense, with White pushing pawns on the queenside and Black pushing pawns on the kingside. You'll notice this is a very closed position. Both sides have eight pawns—the more pawns on the board, the more closed the position. Both sides are one move away from advancing a pawn to open up the game and infiltrate; however, Black's incoming pawn break on the f3 or g3 square is far more dangerous given the proximity to White's king.

When playing in closed positions, you need to think carefully about how to break through your opponent's blockade in an advantageous way and without giving up material unnecessarily.

Summary

Unlike some of the tactical, more forcing concepts you learned in Chapter Seven, strategic play focuses on creating plans of two or more moves, sometimes simply focusing on improving your position rather than securing material gain (although the latter is certainly welcome).

The concept of weaknesses is extremely important, because it is a neat fusion of tactics and strategy. Weaknesses are pieces or squares that have insufficient coverage on them—either completely undefended or defended at most by one piece. As we saw with the examples in this chapter, locating weaknesses and exploiting them the right way could result in an immediately winning position.

Space is the amount of squares your pieces can see on the opponent's side of the board. Naturally, the more space you control, the better your position will be. When you have a dominant space advantage, you restrict the capabilities of your opponent's pieces and can cause lasting damage onto their position. The side with less space should trade off the pieces that are the culprits of their restriction.

Closed positions tend to be locked, where slower maneuvering games occur, or pawn waves like we saw in the King's Indian Defense positions. Open positions, however, are extremely chaotic—you must monitor the diagonals and straightaways, as pieces can see each other from opposite ends of the board.

Follow this QR code to explore some of the strategy concepts in this chapter.

PART TWO 800–1200 ELO

Have you been reading, gradually improving, and are now ready for the next adventure? Or have you picked up this book to scan if the content matches your learning goals? Whatever your situation, I'm excited to dive into some advanced learning together. In Part Two, you will learn how to:

1. Choose the best openings for White and Black in order to win more games

2. Play endgames (the hardest phase of a chess game) like a champion

3. Spot the most common patterns to land spectacular, multi-move combinations

4. Evaluate any chess position correctly

5. Create your own middlegame plans and neutralize your opponents'

Roughly speaking, the readers who will benefit the most from this section will have an Elo between 800 and 1200. If you are below the lower rating, the material may be a bit challenging, but still may be interesting or exciting for you to review. If you are above the maximum, especially if your Elo is 1600–1700, I still think you can learn a good amount and certainly can firm up your skills.

CHAPTER NINE

INTERMEDIATE OPENINGS

In the first few chapters of Part Two, I'm going to give you some insight into my approach to learning chess openings. In Chapters Two and Three, I introduced the basics of openings with both the White and Black pieces; now we're going to layer in some further practical tools to improve your ability to learn and understand openings as you move from a beginner to an intermediate player.

Because there is such a plethora of chess openings, I wanted to introduce in more detail the openings that I recommend for beginners and advanced beginners. A lot of factors go into choosing an opening: your personality, your memory, how lazy you are, how much time you want to dedicate to chess, and your chess style (i.e., if you like solid, principled chess or wild, attacking chess). Based on all those factors, you can choose the openings that suit you best.

Given all those things, I can't know which opening you'd most like to play because I don't know who you are. But I can give you some criteria on how you should choose an opening, and then some practical advice on how to advance your understanding of the opening you've chosen. In this chapter we'll look at some broader considerations that go into choosing openings, which will help you develop your understanding of any opening.

Learning Openings with White

We touched on this in Chapter Two but it's worth repeating here: the first thing to know about chess openings is that you should stick to the same opening as much as possible. Playing the same opening and building your experience within it will deepen your understanding, giving your games familiarity and helping you appreciate the tricks and threats your opening can provide, as well as making you aware of your opponent's best and worst moves against your opening.

To learn openings with White, pick a first move and stick to that first move. Remember what we covered in Chapter Two, though—pick a first move that makes sense and leads to actual studied openings! Playing a flank pawn forward two squares every game would be consistent but also terrible. Instead let's look at d4:

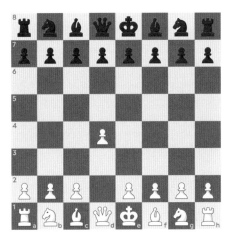

⬆ The Queen's Pawn Opening can lead to the London System, the Queen's Gambit, the Trompowsky Attack, and many other openings. The point is that if you're going play d4, play d4 all the time. Playing a different first move every game just means you never learn any of them in real depth.

Recently I started learning to box, and I fight orthodox, which means I fight with my left hand forward and my right hand back. I've been building my knowledge of boxing on that as a foundation. So if I were to go to the gym tomorrow and suddenly try to fight southpaw—with my right hand forward and left hand back—I wouldn't have a clue what to do. My stance would be wrong, my hands and feet would be confused, and I might fall on my face. All the work I've put in would go out the window. It's similar in chess—give yourself something consistent to build upon. That doesn't have to be d4. It could be e4, the most common first move in chess, which leads to many of the most popular openings. It could be c4, the English, which is a little rarer and trickier to master.

Let's use d4, though, to continue our lesson on how to learn any opening. The laziest—which doesn't mean there's anything wrong with it—continuation of d4 is to play the London System, which is bringing out our dark-squared bishop to f4 and building our pyramid of pawns (see page 34):

⬆ This is the most typical position after two moves in the London. White begins with the queen's pawn (d4), Black responds with d5, and White moves their bishop to f4. Bear in mind that Black might not even play d5, but unless Black plays e5—in which case you'd be able to capture it for free with your d4 pawn—or g5 (in which case just capture the pawn on g5 with your bishop) you can play bishop to f4 on your second move whatever Black does.

From this first position, you can end up in a position—or at least a very similar one—quite often:

⬆ This means that if you start with the London System, you will end up in this kind of position in most of the games you play with White. This makes it something of a "one-size-fits-all" opening as you can play it against most things Black does. Of course, it depends a little bit on how Black plays but in terms of how your pieces are positioned after six moves, this sort of position will become very familiar to you. That means you should be much better prepared in this position than your opponent, who is less likely to know everything about the London System from Black's perspective—because playing with Black means facing a whole range of different White openings.

You don't have to choose the London after d4, of course. We looked briefly at the Queen's Gambit earlier in the book (see page 34). If you want to play the Queen's Gambit then you need to study the best moves against various Black responses. A lot of your moves will be similar and again, a lot of the positions you find yourself in after six or seven moves will be similar. That isn't to say you can play the same few moves in any scenario: clearly if Black would capture one of your pieces on the square you'd ordinarily move to, you need to adapt. The ability to adapt comes from studying the best moves to play based on different moves from Black.

Playing e4, the king's pawn, first is slightly different in that there is no one-size-fits-all opening with e4, as the London would be for d4. Whereas the d4 London System can be played against most things Black does, if you want to play e4 then you need more options in your opening repertoire. In particular, you need to have a plan against Black's two most common responses to e4. First, the symmetrical response:

↑ Here Black has played e5 and you need a plan to continue from here, whether that's the Scotch, the Italian (page 24), or the Spanish Opening (page 30).

Likewise, you'll need a completely different opening plan against the Sicilian Defense (page 25). None of the openings above, like the Scotch or the Ruy López (page 30), work against the Sicilian. The same goes for all the other Black responses to e4 that mean you'll need different ways to play: the Caro-Kann (page 48), the French (page 46), the Modern, the Pirc (page 44), the Scandinavian (page 143), and so on . . . ⬦

You see how chess can become a little bit overwhelming. You can probably also see why I tend to recommend d4 openings for beginners and intermediate players over e4. It might make you wonder why anybody would choose to play openings that elicit such a variety of responses, when the simpler approach might be playing something like the London System, which you can play almost regardless of Black's response. Well, when playing e4, the learning curve might be more intimidating, but you might get a greater variety of positions—which might be more enjoyable for you—as well as deepening your all-around understanding of the game. It's also worth mentioning that certain e4 openings score very highly in terms of win percentages at the beginner and intermediate levels—but they need to be learned carefully, alongside other e4 openings you'll need when the opponent doesn't play how you want them to play.

Learning Openings with Black

When playing with Black, you must be prepared for all of White's possible first moves. That might sound scary but remember that 99 percent of chess games probably start with a small handful of different moves. If White plays trash moves in the opening, refer back to the golden moves (pages 26–28) and take control of the game!

The most common White opening is e4:

⬆ So, the first Black opening you need to prepare will be a response to the King's Pawn. There are lots of choices here, including the Sicilian Defense, the Scandinavian, and the Caro-Kann (page 46), which I play, and which we're going to look at more closely later on.

The challenge when learning Black openings is that you cannot play your e4 response against different first moves for White. For

example, if White plays d4 on the first move, you can no longer play the Sicilian or the Caro-Kann because Queen's Pawn Openings lead to entirely different positions and considerations. And that's before we even consider the Reti, which is White's knight to f3: ⬇

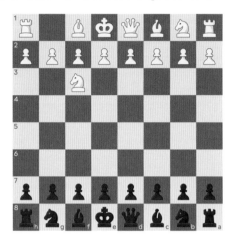

Or the English, White's pawn to c4: ⬇

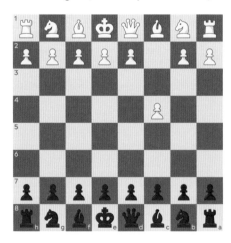

Some people study a specific opening response for each of White's most common openings. Other people don't have the time or the interest in doing that, which is completely understandable.

There's a Black opening we looked at earlier (page 44), the King's Indian or Pirc setup, which can be played pretty much all the time:

⬆ Black puts a pawn on d6, develops their knight to f6, pushes their g pawn one square to allow the bishop to sit on g7, and castles. Theoretically this can be played against almost anything White does—in that sense it's useful for beginners and is a bit like the London System in being a one-size-fits-all approach. Many of the positions you'll find yourself in here with Black will look similar, as will the ideas and game plans associated with the setup.

So, choosing this setup with Black will save you study time because you can play it against almost anything. The downside is that you might find it boring and you may also find this setup just doesn't suit your style of play. If you're losing 70 percent of your games when playing this opening, maybe it isn't for you.

All of these things are part of why it's harder to play chess with Black than it is with White. With White, you can learn one or two openings and play them every game. With Black, there are so many different setups you can play and very often you can find yourself in positions where your opponent is so much better prepared because they've played their opening a thousand times. Clearly you need to learn openings with both White and Black because you have to play both colors (either over the board or online, you won't get to choose). You need to look carefully at Black openings against White's most common responses and choose to study the Black openings that you think suit your play and will be the most challenging for White to deal with. Chess engines, databases, and statistics on whichever online platform you use can really help with learning openings as well as the best moves as the opening progresses.

In the next chapters, we're going to take a deeper dive into an opening for White and an opening for Black that will give you a blueprint for how to practically learn openings. It's worth investigating which openings work at different skill levels, too, no matter your own skill level. It can be educational to study what's common at the levels above your own.

At the highest level of play, there are White and Black openings that are used much more often than others. We call the most common way these games progress "main line," and main line openings at the top level can mean both players knowing the first thirty moves each without even thinking. There is a position in the Najdorf Sicilian, for example, which is 41 moves deep and has appeared hundreds of times at master-level chess.

Given you are very unlikely to be able to play the main lines yet, remember that what works best for grandmasters often isn't what works best for beginners and intermediate players. In the openings we'll look at in the next chapter, my recommendations may not be the main-line or the most popular openings at the top level of chess—and that's because different things make the most sense at the lower levels of chess; plus, if we make less common moves in our openings, then, even if we're facing an opponent who has studied hard, we may take them into less known territory and catch them out.

Let's finish by looking again at the most common opening position after one move each:

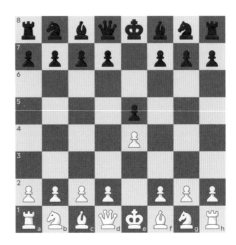

⬆ At an average rating of 1600, this position has been reached 56 million times according to online databases. If we make another move . . .

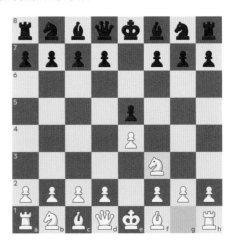

⬆ . . . with knight to f3, we're now down to 35 million of the original 56 million. However, if we play a different move that taps into my approach . . .

♟ . . . by playing knight to c3 instead—the Vienna System—we are in a position that has "only" been reached 3 million times. This shows that studying moves that aren't necessarily the main line at grandmaster level can quickly take games into unfamiliar territory for your opponent—and you can be better prepared to take advantage of that.

In the next chapters I'll give you strong, reputable opening weapons for White and Black that your opponent won't see too often. This is something we'd call a competitive or strategic advantage—you'll hopefully be playing positions that you know better than your opponent, at least in the opening few moves. Of course, I'll just be choosing select examples for each of White and Black, but the same principle applies. Choose an opening and explore how variations that aren't the main lines—but which still score lots of wins—can be played to give yourself an advantage early in a game.

Summary

Depending on various factors, you will need to choose and stick to certain openings for White and Black that suit your playing style, chess strengths, and overall lifestyle. Essentially, if you only have time for thirty minutes of chess on your smartphone during a work break, your opening repertoire should be different than that of a student contending for a national championship. For both White and Black, it's better to know a small number of openings very well than only one or two moves of many different openings.

Follow the QR code to explore more openings with White and Black.

CHAPTER TEN

INTERMEDIATE OPENINGS FOR WHITE

In the previous chapter, I introduced some of the criteria for choosing which openings to play and my philosophy for getting an advantage out of the opening at the intermediate level. Before we continue, it's important to point out that this is not an openings book. You already have a sense of how much preparation is needed to learn specific openings in any depth, which is why there are entire books dedicated solely to individual openings for both White and Black. My aim here is to give you the tools and framework to choose the right openings for you and provide practical ways to advance your understanding of them.

To do that, I'm going to relay my recommendations for White and Black openings that can be very effective as you move into intermediate level, based on my ten-plus years of experience as a chess teacher. You might try what I recommend only for it to fail

in spectacular fashion because it's not a good fit for your personality and style of chess. That's absolutely fine. The main lesson here is to give you a sense of what goes into learning any opening in detail—whether or not you end up playing the examples I use. Learning about your options and then putting them to the test through trial and error (and playing a lot!) will help you sort out what openings work best for you.

London System

Given that we've touched on the London System a couple of times already, you won't be surprised to hear that it's one of my recommendations for opening with the White pieces at the intermediate level. Let's look again at the typical position of a London opening:

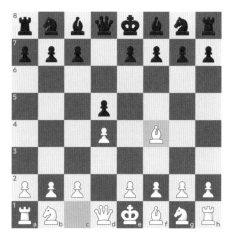

⬆ We put a pawn in the center with d4. Black's most common response here will be d5, preventing us from immediately putting a second pawn in the center. So instead, we play bishop to f4, strengthening our control of the empty e5 square. From here, the position should evolve to look something like the below . . . ⬇

Obviously, there's no guarantee of how Black will set up, but this is what White should be aiming for in a London System. Highlighted is a pyramid of pawns that will prove a tough defense for Black to break through (it's quite a closed position, as covered in Chapter Eight). Our light-squared bishop stands on d3, we've developed our knights toward the center, and we've castled kingside.

So why do I recommend the London? As I've said before, it's the laziest option for White while still being a very effective opening. It requires significantly less study time than other White openings because you can play it against almost anything Black does. As you get more familiar with the London, you'll start adding new spices, the way a chef will begin adding more sophisticated ingredients as they improve at their craft. You'll start picking up certain variations of your move order and piece configuration against suboptimal moves Black plays.

 FUN FACT

In the three-year span from January 2020 to January 2023, the London System has been played over 20 million times in online chess games.

Black has only one possible way to prevent you playing the London, which is to play e5 on the first move: ⬇

This is called the Englund Gambit and it prevents us moving the bishop out to f4. But it is also a free pawn. White can capture the Black pawn on e5 and from there White should develop naturally, bringing the knights out to c3 and f3 and moving our bishops to the center (using the golden moves we looked at in Chapter Two). With logical play, the Englund Gambit isn't a good move and just leaves Black down a pawn. You can learn the full refutation of the England Gambit by using the QR code at the end of this chapter.

But it's worth noting that there are reasons that Black plays the Englund Gambit. Specifically, there are a couple of particularly nasty traps Black can spring based on the Englund Gambit—which can result in you losing your queen—so you need to explore these with a chess engine and study how to stop them. But if you do learn the very simple ways to avoid the Englund Gambit traps, you'll just be much better after one move of the game. The Englund Gambit isn't a good choice for Black if White knows what they're doing.

Black could also attempt to prevent the London by playing c5:

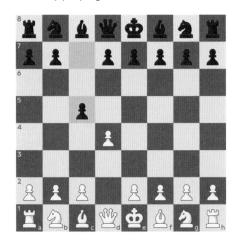

⬆ This is certainly a tricky move, trying to dislodge your central pawn. Capturing the c5 pawn is worse for White than capturing on e5 like in the England Gambit.

White can stick to the plan and still play bishop to f4, knowing Black might capture the d4 pawn, or . . .

. . . play c3, bolstering the central pawn and continuing to build the pawn pyramid before potentially playing bishop to f4 on the next move—depending on whether Black captures the d4 pawn or leaves it. ⬇

So, as you can see, it's almost impossible for your opponent to stop you from playing your London in a very similar way from game to game—which is why I like the London. You can also see, however, that even against the London—the most difficult White opening for Black to prevent—there are a couple of things Black can do very early on that get in your way. The same is true for move two, move three, and so on. So, whichever opening you choose, sit down with an openings book or chess engine and explore the best options against Black's moves at different stages of the opening. After studying, the next part is to play lots of games and gain experience of

different Black responses. Even when you lose games, analyze them afterward to see what went wrong in the opening (or if you played perfectly). As with learning anything, repetition and reflection will help deepen your understanding of your chosen opening.

Going back to the London, the most effective way for Black to play against it is, at some point, to play c5:

⬆ The reason c5 is so useful for Black when playing against the London is that it opens up the Black queen's diagonal, especially the b6 square, where it can target the undefended White pawn on b2. Black playing c5 also threatens to deflect our d4 pawn off the center, destabilizing our pyramid. So, what should White do if Black plays c5? White . . .

. . . should play c3. If Black captures the d4 pawn, we recapture with our c or e pawn. ⬇

From here Black may continue with their plan to bring the queen to b6, at which point White has a few options to defend against this. The QR code at the end of this chapter will take you through the London in more detail—for now, it's important to see how much studying can go into even the most one-size-fits-all opening for White! Studying and practicing are the only ways to improve your openings.

Vienna System

My second recommendation when playing White is to start with e4. There are certain pros and cons that come with playing e4 instead of the London (d4), some of which we've already touched upon. The pros of e4 are increased variety in the positions you can get, and in e4 games there are situations where you can be completely winning in the first ten moves (even if your opponent plays sensible-looking moves). That is not something the London ordinarily offers, apart from situations where your opponent has blundered their queen—which has more to do with their playing like a bozo than it does your opening. With e4, if you know the main lines— what we call the "theory"—you can achieve winning positions in ten moves.

The downside of playing e4 is that Black has six or seven opening moves that respond to it, all of which are decent and for which you need to be prepared. At the advanced beginner and intermediate level, the way to study e4 is to study Black's two most common response moves. After that we'll look at some of the overarching theory associated with e4 games.

The most common move against e4 is of course e5:

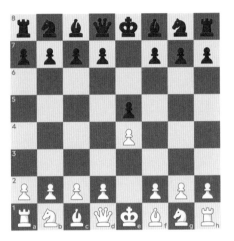

⬆ We've seen this a few times now. Usually White develops their kingside knight to f3 and enters an Italian or Spanish Opening, but here I'm going to recommend a less common second move, which is . . .

. . . knight to c3. This is known as the Vienna System. The Vienna System is one of the highest-scoring openings at the beginner and intermediate level because it's easy to understand and comes with some powerful traps if Black isn't careful. ⬇

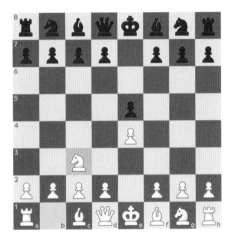

♔ FUN FACT

According to my chess.com database, I have played the Vienna 450 times (at the time of this writing, in November 2022) and I have a 70 percent win rate. I believe in the Vienna against some of the best grandmasters in the world, so naturally I recommend it to you, dear reader!

⬆ Black's most natural response to the Vienna System is knight to f6. In response, we immediately strike . . .

⬆ . . . with f4. This is known as the Vienna Gambit because we are gambiting a pawn (i.e., we are giving it up for "free"). If Black takes the pawn on f4, White pushes the pawn to e5, after which the win rate for White shoots up to 64 percent.

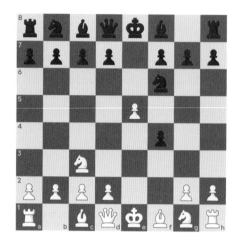

⬆ Remember that ordinarily White wins about 50 percent of the time, so this is impressive. According to online databases, this position has occurred more than 1 million times, so it's a significant sample size, too.

The reason this position is so strong for White is that Black's best next move is to retreat the knight back to g8, where it started, lest it be captured by the lower-value pawn. ⬇

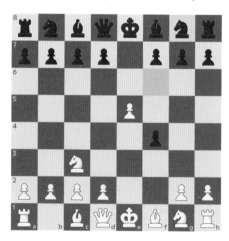

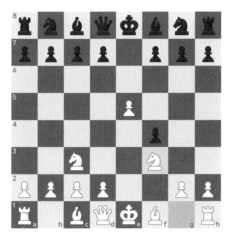

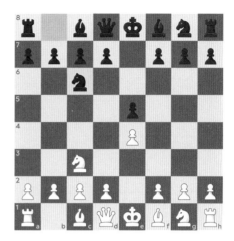

⬆ Next, White should play knight to f3, preventing the Black queen from playing a dangerous check on the h4 square while also developing a piece. White completely dominates the center in this position and has two pieces developed, while Black has none. White is still down a pawn but can win it back easily by playing d4 on the next move, allowing the dark-squared bishop to attack Black's pawn on f4.

Again, there will be a QR code at the end of this chapter for exploring the Vienna in much greater detail, but for now you can see how playing a less common approach to e4 positions can be very dangerous to your opponent at the beginner and intermediate level. This is why I love the Vienna Gambit—unless Black knows what they're doing, you can be winning very quickly. There's another variation I like in the Vienna:

⬆ Let's say that Black chooses to mirror White's position by playing knight to c6 on move two. And let's say Black continues to mirror our moves . . .

⬆ . . . by playing bishop to c5 after we've played bishop to c4. There is a move here for White that wins for White 63 percent of the time, which is . . .

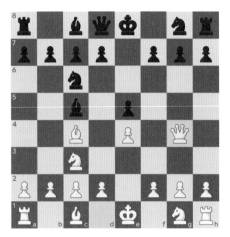

♟ . . . queen to g4. This attacks Black's pawn on g7 and threatens to trap Black's rook after capturing the pawn. So Black has to be very careful here, and we're only four moves into the game!

These two weapons in the Vienna could conceivably boost your win rate significantly, which is amazing and one of the reasons the Vienna System is worth learning. I highly encourage it to both beginners and inter-mediates. Use the QR code at the end of the chapter to explore it further.

Alapin Sicilian Variation

If you play e4, the second most common move you need to be prepared for is the Sicilian Defense, which is when Black plays pawn to c5 in response to e4. I don't recommend the Sicilian to beginners and intermediates because it's enormously complicated, but it doesn't mean your opponents will follow that advice—they might play it because they've seen Magnus Carlsen do it and think they should copy him. Also, please keep in mind that this is simply my opinion. I am one per-son, one coach. Other people may disagree, to the extent that they *only* tell their students to play the Sicilian. Coaching philosophies are all different, but you are holding my book, after all, so you'll be getting my thoughts. The first thing to point out here is that once your opponent plays the Sicilian in response to your e4, the Vienna System no longer works. You can only play the Vienna against Black's pawn to e5; if you try to implement your Vienna ideas and tricks against anything other than e5, they won't work, and you may end up in a bad position very quickly.

There are many ways for White to play against the Sicilian, but my recommendation is to play c3:

♟ The intention behind playing c3 is to play d4 on the next move—putting two pawns in the center and challenging Black's c5 pawn. This is known as the Alapin Variation of the Sicilian. It's basically a way to remove 90 percent of the study time your opponent has put into the Sicilian, because they won't face the Alapin too often.

Black's two most popular responses in this position—making up about 53 percent of games played online—are:

♟ knight to c6,

♟ and d6, which has been played about half as much as knight to c6 above. When White plays d4 after either of these variations, they statistically score very well in terms of wins.

I really like the Alapin and it is my main recommendation against the Sicilian Defense. The Vienna and Alapin are great tools against Black's most common responses to e4 and I would definitely recommend studying them further if you want to play e4 with White—again by using opening-specific databases or books, chess engines, and by practicing them in games.

Of course, Black doesn't have to play either e5 or c5 in response to e4 or d4. In Chapter Three we looked at building-block openings like the French Defense and the Caro-Kann. Against both, I recommend the advance variations.

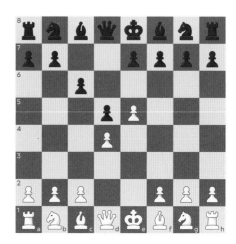

⬆ The Advance Variation of the Caro-Kann Defense is very similar—when Black attacks the center, rather than capture we push our e pawn forward.

In both cases, pushing the e pawn forward restricts your opponent's space and makes it more difficult for them to develop. At the beginner and intermediate level, players often struggle with a lack of space, so choking off your opponent's pieces can force them into making rash moves to fight back. Your opponent has to spend time breaking open your center while you are able to quickly develop, bolstering your central blockade. Still, there are ways that Black can strike back against the advance variations of both the French and Caro-Kann and undermine your blockade, so you should study how to handle various Black responses.

⬆ In the Advance Variation of the French Defense, White has put two pawns in the center, Black has attacked the center with d5 and instead of White capturing, we push our e pawn forward to e5.

Summary

In Chapter Ten, we went over my opening recommendations for the White pieces. In order to successfully start chess games with 1. e4, the King's Pawn Opening, you must know how to challenge every major Black defense (symmetrical e5, Sicilian, French, Caro-Kann, Scandinavian, Modern) and be ready to dedicate some hours of study to building a thorough opening repertoire.

The Vienna and Alapin are my suggestions against Black's two most popular responses, because they lead to predictable positions with straightforward plans. Other suggestions can be found, as always, at the QR code at the end of the chapter.

If you choose to start with 1. d4, the Queen's Pawn Opening, I believe the London System is the way to go. Your setup in the first ten moves will look nearly identical, thereby saving you hours of opening study, and you can build up your experience by playing many practice games with this opening.

Before we move on, allow me to emphasize that these recommendations are based on my own history of playing and teaching. You do not need to take my word as some almighty chess whisperer—if you enjoy playing your own openings successfully with the White pieces, I can only be happy for you. However, given that you are currently holding the book that I authored, I figured it would make sense to tell you exactly what openings *I think* you should play to win more games of chess!

 Follow this QR code to explore various intermediate White openings in more depth.

CHAPTER ELEVEN

INTERMEDIATE OPENINGS FOR BLACK

Now let's look in more detail at what I find to be the most effective openings for Black at the intermediate level. These are the Black openings that I find to be the easiest to learn and play but which also follow my philosophy of quickly departing the main lines and taking our opponents out of their comfort zone. Even though you're playing with Black, you can quickly be the one doing the attacking from early on if you're better prepared than your opponent.

We've previously touched on how much trickier it is to be prepared when playing with Black, because White has lots of options for their first move. But we can start by preparing for White's most common openings and progress from there. We're going to look at defenses against e4 and d4—notably e4 is 2.5 times as popular as d4, and combined e4 and d4 openings will constitute 90–95 percent of the games you're going to play. So being prepared against these two openings is crucial. You can either have an opening prepared against each or play a universal setup against both, which we'll cover later in the chapter.

Scandinavian Defense

I have two recommendations for playing against e4, and I recommend that you continuously play whichever one you choose (if you like either) rather than switching between the two, as you'll deepen your understanding and appreciation that way. My first recommendation against e4 is to play d5, the Scandinavian Defense.

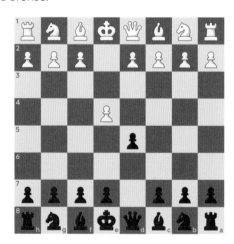

⬆ This immediately forces our opponent to make a decision (whether to capture our d5 pawn or not), which is why I like the Scandinavian. Usually, White is forcing the opening and Black is responding but this defense forces White into our game plan. Typically, White will capture our d5 pawn and we will recapture with our queen . . .

⬆ . . . to give us this position. You'll notice that this breaks some of the opening principles we looked at earlier on (i.e., not bringing the queen out early), but in this case there's a way to play it correctly that results in a strong position for Black. White does have a very natural and dangerous-looking third move . . .

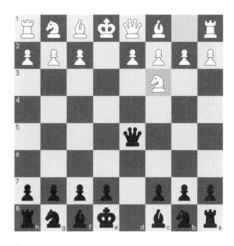

⬆ . . . which is knight to c3, attacking our queen and forcing Black to move it again. Whenever this happens, we respond by . . .

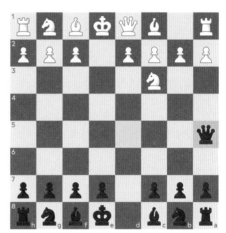

⬆ . . . rotating our queen to a5, making it difficult for White to immediately attack our queen again.

The reason I like the Scandinavian is that it's forcing in nature. We attack White's central pawn with our first move, recapture with the queen, and suddenly White is playing Black's game. Black's game plan from the previous position is to develop our knights and bishops and castle our king. When playing the Scandinavian, there is another important move to remember:

⬆ The move c6 allows the Black queen to escape to either c7 or d8 if White finds a way to attack it again. You can play the move c6 as early as this or just have it in mind if you sense White is maneuvering their pieces to target your queen.

From here Black develops naturally and should end up in a position something like the following diagram:

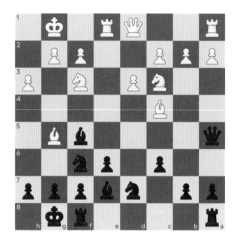

⬆ All our pieces have been developed from their starting positions to active squares, our position is rock solid, and our queen is very active—but still has that escape route if attacked.

There is no way for White to immediately punish the Scandinavian Defense if played correctly, which makes it a great opening for Black to play against e4. The Scandinavian Defense is a good Black opening for beginners and intermediates because it's straightforward to learn, will result in relatively consistent positions across your games, and your opponents will probably face it less often than other e4 defenses (like e5, the Sicilian, the Caro-Kann, or the French). Your opponent would probably need to know 15–20 moves of chess computer theory to come out of the opening with a meaningful advantage against the Scandinavian, which is very unlikely and means you should be in a good position heading into the middlegame.

The main drawback of the Scandinavian is that you are putting your queen out in the center of the board on the second move, so the danger is always there that you'll lose your queen by not moving it to safe squares. Remember to slide the queen over to a5 and remember to give your queen the escape route with c6 as soon as possible. After that, finish your development and you should be in a strong position to do battle with White.

Caro-Kann Defense

My second recommendation is my favorite opening even at the International Master level. I have beaten close to a hundred grandmasters with this opening and it is of course the Caro-Kann Defense. The Caro-Kann can only be played against e4 and it begins with c6:

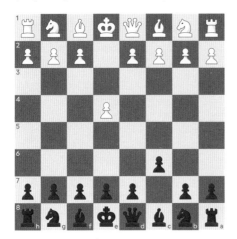

⬆ The point of this opening from Black's perspective is to put a pawn in the center but have it protected by another pawn—what we call a building-block opening. So, when White puts two pawns in the center . . .

. . . we play d5. We played d5 immediately in the Scandinavian, but in this case we play d5 after we've prepared its protection with the c pawn. If White captures, we can recapture with our pawn. ⬇

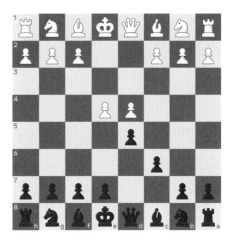

At the end of the chapter there will be a QR code that links to a more in-depth online lesson on the Caro-Kann, but for now I'll say the reason I like this opening so much is that we're again forcing White into making a decision of whether to capture our d pawn or not. Notice how we are also attacking White's e pawn—it isn't defended so we are forcing White into action and wresting control of the opening from them. From the above position, the Caro-Kann develops in three different ways depending on whether White pushes their e pawn to e5 (the Advance Variation), captures our d pawn (the Exchange Variation), or defends their e pawn, with either another pawn or other piece.

Against the Advance Variation, which looks like this: ↓

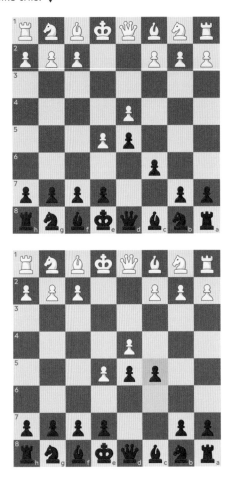

Black should respond by pushing the c pawn to c5. This is a sacrifice of the c pawn but undermines White's center, knocking White's d pawn off center and making both White's pawns vulnerable to capture. In online game databases, this position already scores more wins for Black than it does for White, which is pretty astounding after just three moves. If you study and prepare a few moves beyond this, you'll probably find yourself winning 60 percent or more of your games with Black when this position occurs, because White has to be very precise to avoid various traps as the Advance Variation proceeds.

Let's go back and say that White defends the e pawn instead of pushing it:

In this situation—or any situation where White defends the e pawn—we are simply going to capture it . . .

... with our d pawn, at which point White ... ⬇

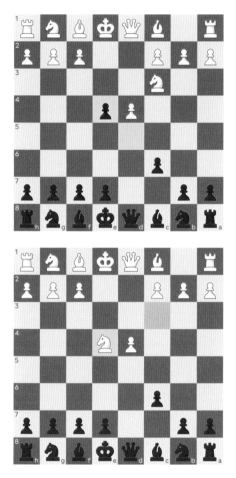

⬆ ... will recapture. Now White no longer has two pawns in the center. In this position, Black can play ...

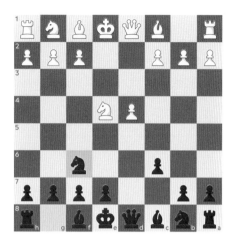

⬆ ... knight to f6, offering a trade of knights. This is another line of the Caro-Kann that needs to be studied in more detail, but already Black is doing fine in this position. Likewise, if White does capture the Black knight on f6, Black has the option of recapturing with either the e or g pawn—which requires more study to find out the best moves afterward.

The third choice Black has in the Caro-Kann is the Exchange Variation, which is when White immediately captures our d5 pawn with their e pawn. Black then recaptures and the position looks like this:

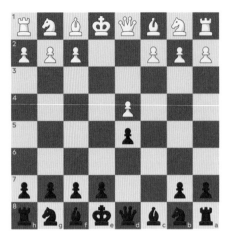

 Again, this is good for Black. White doesn't have two pawns in the center. From here, we develop our knights and bishops to natural squares, castle our king, and play chess.

In my opinion the Caro-Kann is an amazing weapon that can be used from the beginner to world champion level. It's an opening I've used throughout my career and one that has a special place in my heart. Between the ages of twelve and fifteen I actually quit chess, not playing at all after spending my entire childhood at a chessboard. There were a few reasons why I'd quit—partly because of the difficult teenage phase, partly because of problems at school, with friends, and at home.

A lot of things were tough in those years and my chess naturally suffered because of that. When I came back to chess as a fifteen-year-old, the first book I picked up was Lars Schandorff's *Grandmaster Repertoire 7: The Caro-Kann*, which had been recommended by one of my closest friends. After learning this opening, I went on to beat my first National Master, who was rated 2200, before gaining rating points in my next fifteen tournaments, reaching 2200 and gaining the National Master title for myself. You could argue I might have gotten it three years earlier if I hadn't quit playing, but who knows. In any case, the Caro-Kann has held a dear place in my heart ever since for saving my life (at least my chess life).

♚ **FUN FACT**

The strongest grandmaster I ever defeated was Hikaru Nakamura, formerly ranked number two in the world, and I did it in the Caro-Kann Defense. You can check out that game by following the QR code at the end of the chapter!

Queen's Gambit Declined

Now that we've looked at my two recommendations for playing against e4, what about against White's second most popular move, d4? Like the Sicilian, the Scandinavian and Caro-Kann can only be played against e4. Trying to play them against d4 or any other White opening would quickly result in serious problems!

D4 is a slower opening in nature than e4 and can include the London and the Queen's Gambit from White's perspective. All of these openings involve a slower approach to development for White, which means when playing Black that there are fewer immediate traps to fall into.

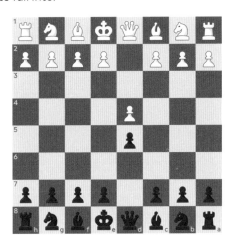

⬆ Against d4 I really like the Queen's Gambit Declined setup for Black. We begin by playing d5, mirroring White. If White then plays . . .

. . . c4—the Queen's Gambit—we decline capturing the free pawn on c4 and instead . . . ⬇

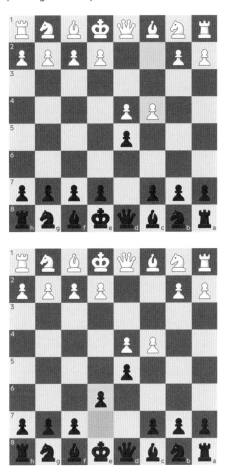

⬆ . . . play e6. This way we defend our central pawn and keep a pawn in the center. If White captures our d5 pawn, we recapture with our e pawn.

From here we develop our knights and bishops on the kingside and castle our king, ending up in a position something like this:

⬆ Here we've still got a central presence with pawns, pieces developed, and a very safe king. Since we've blocked in our light-squared bishop (i.e., our pawn on e6 stops our bishop from moving to one of its natural squares on f5 or g4), instead we should play b6 so that on our next move . . . ⬇

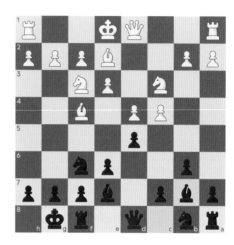

⬆ . . . we can position our bishop on b7. Here our bishop adds extra support to our pawn on d5 and would also be strongly placed on the diagonal if the center ever opens up when pawns get traded off.

Again, this will be a relatively consistent position you get in Queen's Gambit games and it's a fairly straightforward defense to learn with the Black pieces. Of course, White doesn't have to play the Queen's Gambit after d4, and they may make unusual moves that take the game into unfamiliar territory for both players, but this sort of setup for Black should mostly be possible in *any* game where White doesn't start with e4. So, it's not just d4 openings but also c4 (the English) or knight to f3 (the Reti) where Black can consistently aim for a position that looks like this:

♟ This is more or less the position you'll be consistently shooting for against every White opening that isn't e4. Your c and d pawns are farthest forward, supported by the b and e pawns. Your king is safely castled, your knights are developed, and your bishops sit on the e7 and b7 squares, supporting your pawns and well placed for when the board opens up.

Setup-Based Openings

There are a few setups for Black that can be played almost universally, meaning that if you master them, you won't need to learn a different Black opening against e4 and non-e4 openings—this would suit players who don't want to, or don't have time, to learn multiple openings in depth. This is what I mean by "setup-based openings"—you are prepared with a setup that you can play regardless of how the opponent responds.

The King's Indian/Pirc and the Dutch are two setup-based openings that can be played

very consistently—the King's Indian/Pirc against anything and the Dutch against anything except e4. The drawback of setup-based openings is that Black tends to be more passive. The reason for that is that you cannot be aggressive when playing one of these setups. You can't fight for central space and active development because when your opponent challenges your extended pieces, you will likely have to respond by moving or trading pieces, which will disrupt the setup you're building toward. Playing setup-based openings is like being a counterpuncher in boxing or MMA; you have a fixed defensive setup and you are rarely the aggressor, instead responding to what your opponent throws at you and picking your moment to counterattack. You won't be looking for a dynamic, crazy range of attacks but rather react to what's thrown at you.

We've briefly touched on the King's Indian or Pirc Defense, which looks like this:

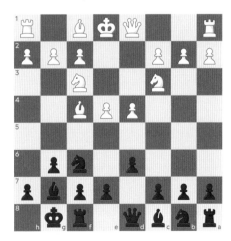

You can play this against literally any of White's main openings. Black puts a pawn on d6, pushes the g pawn to g6, puts the bishop on g7, moves the knight to f6, and castles. It's important to note the Black pawn on d6: this is a crucial move in the King's Indian because it prevents White from pushing their e pawn and attacking our knight on f6.

There is another setup Black can use in all cases *except* against e4, which is the Dutch Defense:

↑ The Dutch Defense begins with the move f5, which is a practical opening move because it fights for the center in a different way (a pawn on f5 prevents White putting a second pawn on e4). The reason you can't play this against e4 is that White will simply be able to capture your f5 pawn, but otherwise you can play the Dutch against everything White does.

As with all openings, the Dutch needs to be studied because there are different variations and ways the defense progresses depending on White's play. One is the Leningrad Variation, which looks like this:

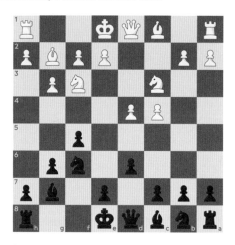

↑ You'll notice this resembles the King's Indian except that we have the f pawn pushed up to f5. The drawback of this opening is that, as early as the first move, you are weakening your king by pushing the pawns in front of it and leaving gaps for enemy pieces to see and move through.

Another variation of the Dutch looks like this:

⬆ This is a different type of Dutch Defense. The Black king is a little safer here and the dark-squared bishop is out in the open rather than fianchettoed on g7 (a **fianchetto** is the technical name for putting the bishop on g7 or b7 for Black, and b2 or g2 for White). In this variation, the e pawn has been pushed forward instead of the d or g pawn. Again, there are positives and negatives to this variation of the Dutch Defense—if it's a setup that appeals to you then you should study the different lines and explore what works best in different situations.

Summary

Half of your games will be played with the Black pieces, and about 90 percent of those games will begin with 1. e4 or 1. d4. My philosophy from the previous chapter remains the same: choose an opening, stick to it, and build your experience in the ensuing positions.

Against 1. e4, I prefer the Scandinavian or Caro-Kann Defenses. The plans are straightforward and the possible deviations by the opponent are quite limited. The former is a bit riskier than the latter due to the early sortie by the queen, so you are welcome to choose which flavor of opening you prefer.

Against 1. d4—and the London or the Queen's Gambit—I believe in principled, central-pawn play. Remember that your d pawn and c pawn are best friends and generally like to come out together, if possible.

Setup-based defenses are a fantastic way to cut back on study time and have consistent positions in the early stage of the game. The King's Indian/Pirc and Dutch Defenses are universal options of natural development.

Follow this **QR code** to explore these recommended Black openings in more detail.

CHAPTER TWELVE
GAMBITS

Before we leave openings, it's important to look at gambits. The word *gambit* comes from the Italian word *gambetto*, which is the act of tripping someone with the leg to make them fall. As far as chess goes, you will not be physically assaulting your opponent. Rather, a gambit in chess is when a player sacrifices material—a pawn—with the aim of achieving a subsequent positional advantage or, at times, immediate knockout victory via checkmate as early as move seven or eight.

It's important to understand that, while winning that quickly sounds great, gambits come in all shapes and sizes, and most don't offer instant victory. Most gambits merely give you a positional edge for the momentary loss of a pawn, and typically there will be ways to quickly win your pawn back. That's if your opponent even captures the free pieces you're offering; gambits can either be accepted or declined, which we'll look at in more detail in this chapter. Some gambits are gambits only in name, meaning the opponent can accept them and there is no huge risk involved.

Other gambits are extremely dangerous to accept—you need to be aware of these from both an attacking and a defending point of view. Some gambits are also very risky for the person playing the gambit, not just because you are giving up a pawn but because gambit positions are usually high-risk, high-reward scenarios. If all the tricks and traps associated with the gambit don't work (because the opponent is aware of them and knows how to defend), you'll probably be in a bad position and down material with nothing to show for it.

Gambits are fun things to add to your toolbox and important to know so you don't fall into the traps when your opponent plays them against you. Really, gambits should be sprinkled into your repertoire rather than forming the basis of how you play every game. In chess, like in life, everything should be in moderation. You can enjoy something sweet now and then, but your diet shouldn't be entirely sugar (for legal reasons, I should say I'm not a doctor or a nutritionist; I'll stick to giving advice on chess).

Gambits for White

Roughly 90 percent of gambits for White begin with e4, the King's Pawn Opening:

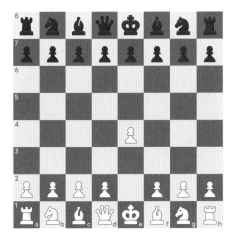

↑ That's because it's the most "open" move, by which I mean you open up a way out for both your queen and bishop at the same time. We know this is the most common opening and there are more tactics associated with e4 than d4. One of the most legendary gambits in chess . . .

. . . occurs after Black responds with e5 and White . . . ⬇

↑ . . . plays f4. This is the King's Gambit. White is sacrificing a pawn and simultaneously opening up the king on the dark-squared diagonal.

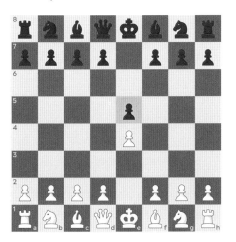

↑ If Black accepts the gambit by taking on f4, White then . . .

. . . plays knight to f3. This develops a piece but also prevents Black from playing a dangerous queen check on h4. White can now take control of the center . . . ⬇

⬆ . . . by moving out their d pawn. In the next few moves, White can easily develop their bishops (notice that in this position our dark-squared bishop is threatening to capture the Black pawn on f4, so Black will have to give it up or waste time defending it), bring out the queenside knight and castle the king. So even though White has given up a pawn, White has compensation in the form of central control and quick development.

The King's Gambit dominated chess until the late nineteenth century during what we call the Romantic era of chess. One of the most famous and beautiful chess games ever played, the so-called Immortal Game between Adolf Anderssen and Lionel Kieseritzky in 1851, began with a King's Gambit. If you've never seen the Immortal Game, google it: White wins despite sacrificing half his pieces and being down an incredible 21 points of material. During the Romantic era players would often sacrifice lots of material to win games in the flashiest possible ways, which probably explains why the King's Gambit was so popular.

Accepting the King's Gambit in the pre-computer era was often too dangerous, but nowadays Black—with best play—can equalize the position pretty comfortably. At the beginner and intermediate level, you won't come across best play too often, making the King's Gambit a dangerous weapon and something your opponents won't likely be prepared for.

There are many gambits in e4 e5 positions—this way we wrap up coverage of symmetrical kings pawn positions—but now let's look at another gambit, this time in the "other" direction:

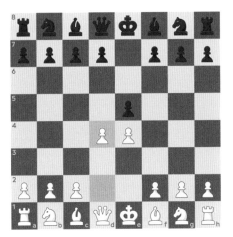

⬆ This is known as the Danish Gambit. White opens with e4, Black responds with e5, and White then plays d4.

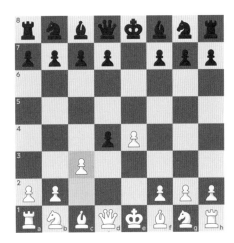

⬆ . . . with the move c3.

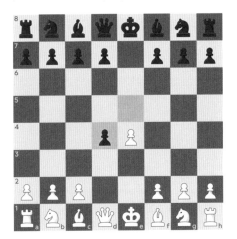

⬆ If Black takes the d4 pawn, White may gambit *another* pawn . . .

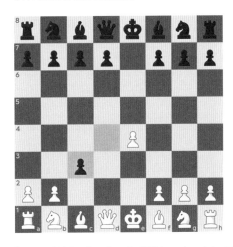

⬆ And if Black takes it, White should still not capture back and instead play . . .

⬆ . . . bishop to c4.

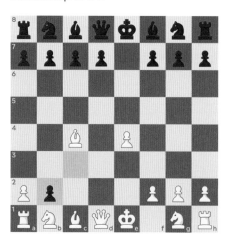

⬆ If Black keeps chomping pawns, capturing b2, White will finally take the pawn back with the move . . .

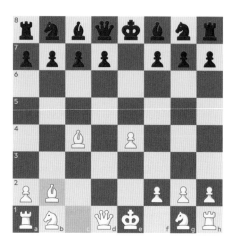

⬆ . . . bishop takes b2. White has lost three pawns for Black's one, but White has two active, powerful bishops on the diagonal and Black has no pieces out at all. White could play queen to b3 on the next move, forming a battery with the bishop and targeting Black's weak f7 pawn.

The Danish Gambit is one of the most exciting openings in chess. Like other openings, use a chess engine to study the best moves depending on how Black plays. They may not keep capturing the pawns you offer, for example. In games played online, the above position leads to a White win roughly 60 percent of the time—that shows how dangerous a position it is for Black to defend, especially when Black is unprepared for it.

There are gambits that can be played against other major openings, too. For example, against the Sicilian Defense.

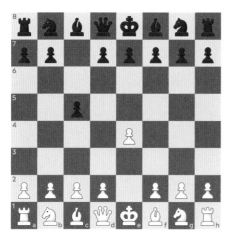

⬆ We know this is Black's second most common response to e4. White has a gambit here . . .

⬆ . . . then White uses a similar strategy as in the Danish Gambit, with the move c3 . . .

⬆ . . . with the move d4. If Black captures d4 . . .

⬆ . . . if Black captures the c3 pawn, White should retake with . . .

♟ . . . the knight. This is called the Smith-Morra Gambit. Here White is down a pawn but has open lines to develop their pieces, while Black has no pieces or pawns out at all. Fast-forward a few natural moves and the position can look like this:

🖊 White is still a pawn down, but all their pieces are out, the king is safely castled, and Black's position is relatively cramped and lacking space. Black's bishops are multiple moves away from getting into good positions, which also prevents Black from castling. So, for the cost of one pawn White has better development, a safer king, and more space.

Some gambits are therefore dangerous for Black to accept. We looked at the Vienna Gambit earlier (page 136), which can be particularly dangerous for Black if they don't know what they're doing. Black should not accept the Vienna Gambit because White can use it to get to a very strong position very quickly.

Let's not forget our favorite chess-themed Netflix series, too, *The Queen's Gambit*. Here's the actual gambit:

♟ This is hardly even considered a gambit, since the move c4 (the gambiting move) is the most popular in this position.

The Queen's Gambit Accepted isn't imme-diately losing for Black, but once White plays . . .

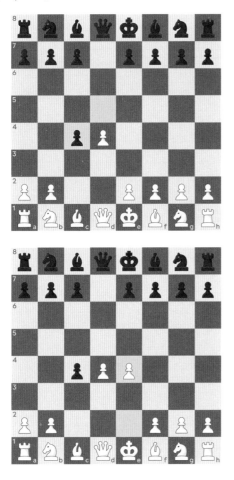

 . . . e4, Black has surrendered full con-trol of the center *and* White's light-squared bishop attacks Black's pawn on c4. I do not recommend accepting the Queen's Gambit when playing with Black—surrendering control of the center at beginner and inter-mediate level is very dangerous.

The Queen's Gambit is therefore one of those gambits that are only really a gambit in name. White is technically giving up a pawn but the position after the Queen's Gambit Accepted is usually better and not risky for White at lower levels of play. The Queen's Gambit has been played as an opening for centuries and has survived the arrival of chess computers, which haven't exposed it as a fatally flawed opening the way it has with other openings from centuries past. Playing the Queen's Gambit with White is therefore a decent overall opening, whether Black accepts the gambit or not. If Black declines the gambit, develop your knights and bishops and castle as per the golden moves from Chapter One.

♔ **FUN FACT**

Based on games played online, the Danish Gambit is the most successful White gambit at club level, winning nearly 60 percent of the time.

Gambits for Black

The first thing to say here is that playing gambits with Black is significantly more risky than playing them with White. Playing second in chess is already a disadvantage; when you add the loss of material to that, you have to be very careful about what you're getting yourself into. Gambits with Black are extremely high risk, high reward. Gambits with White generally lead to aggressive positions and quick development. Gambits with Black tend to either lose or win. That's it. There's very little in between.

If you're comfortable with that, then I'm going to introduce a couple of Black gambits that can be very effective. Let's start with this position:

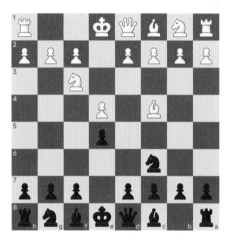

✏ This is the Italian Game and a pretty common position after White has played e4 and Black has responded with e5. In fact, it's been reached over 200 million times in online games. Here Black can play . . .

↑ . . . knight to d4. This is the Blackburne Shilling Gambit, which has been played only 500,000 times out of the 9 million games featuring the above position—roughly 5 percent of the games. This position is losing for Black if White simply captures the Black knight with their own knight and continues natural development. But for some opponents, it will be very tempting to play . . .

↑ . . . knight takes e5. Free pawn, right? Well, Black responds by immediately playing . . .

↑ . . . by playing knight takes f7. Not only does that capture another pawn, but it forks Black's queen and rook. Which is bad, except Black . . .

↑ . . . queen to g5. That attacks both White's knight in the center and White's pawn on g2. From here, many people playing White will continue the knight's journey . . .

↑ . . . captures White's pawn on g2. Black has won a pawn back and now attacks White's rook in the corner as well as White's pawn on e4. White will very likely play . . .

♟ . . . rook to f1 here to prevent the queen from capturing the rook (Black's king now defends it).

Black will . . .

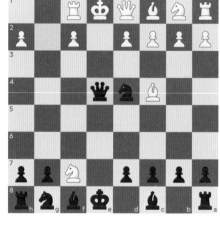

♟ . . . gobble the pawn on e4 with check. The White king cannot move. If White blocks with the queen, Black will take it with the knight and is up a queen. So instead White might play the more natural move of . . .

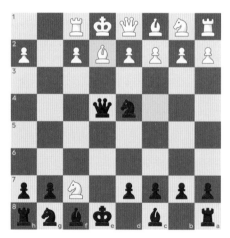

♟ . . . blocking with the bishop. But there is one final, nasty trick here.

♚ **FUN FACT**

According to the Lichess database, the Blackburne Shilling Gambit trap has worked over 400,000 times, even against 2800-Elo players (albeit in bullet, or 1-minute chess).

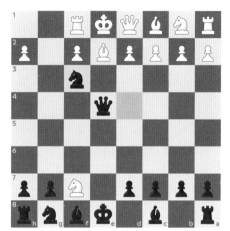

⬆ Black plays knight to f3. Not only is that check—it is in fact checkmate. And Black has gotten there in just *seven* moves. White's king cannot move, and the bishop cannot capture the knight because it's pinned to the White king by the Black queen. At the 1600 average Elo, 18,000 games have gone like this. So White does fall for it in the real world!

Of course, there are a lot of moves White has to make for this gambit to pay off for Black. Knight to d4 is a bluff, and just like in poker, if your bluff gets called when you have a bad hand then you're going to lose money. If your bluff gets called in chess, you're going to be in a bad position. The Blackburne Shilling Gambit can literally win you the game in seven moves. But as you climb the ratings ladder, this is not going to work—opponents will be wise to the tricks and traps of this position and punish you for trying it.

Another example of a Black gambit that wins in eight moves is the Englund Gambit:

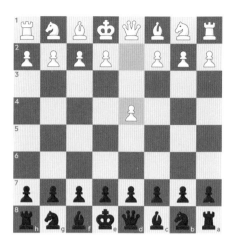

⬆ This gambit is a response to the Queen's Pawn Opening, d4.

⬆ In response, Black plays e5. Let's say White takes that e5 pawn and Black attacks the White pawn with . . .

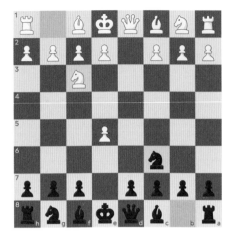

♟ . . . knight to c6, at which point White defends the pawn with knight to f3.

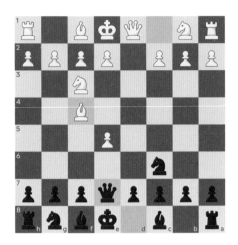

♟ Black then adds an attacker with queen to e7. White adds another defender of the pawn with bishop to f4. Here Black has a very dangerous move, which is . . .

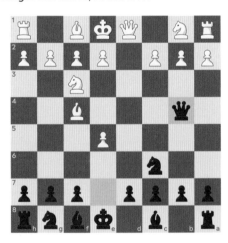

♟ . . . queen to b4 check. The Black queen is attacking three things at the same time here: the White king (meaning White has to deal with the check), the White bishop on f4, and the White pawn on b2.

♟ White will likely try to deal with two of these threats at once by playing bishop back to d2. So Black will . . .

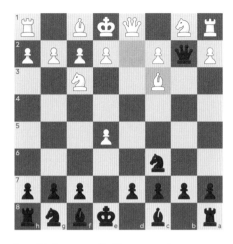

♟ . . . bishop to c3. That attacks our queen and prevents the queen from taking the rook in the corner. But here Black uncorks the trick with the move . . .

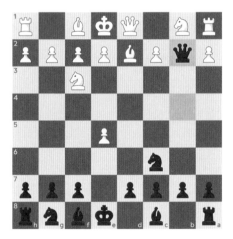

♟ . . . grab the pawn, which also threatens to capture the White rook on a1. The best move is knight to c3, but White may try to save the rook by playing . . .

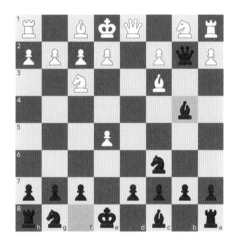

♟ . . . bishop to b4. This pins the White bishop to the king, meaning it can no longer capture the Black queen. And Black is threatening to capture the bishop with their own bishop.

⬆ So, a natural move by White is to move the queen to d2, adding more defense to the White bishop. But after Black takes the White bishop with their own bishop and the White queen recaptures . . .

⬆ . . . Black makes the move queen to c1, which is checkmate.

You'll see how several things have to go right for Black to be able to deliver this checkmate. There are a series of specific responses White has to make for all of this to work. And there are opportunities along the way for White to instead play the best moves—many of White's moves shown above look natural but are not the best—and basically refute the entire gambit, leaving Black in a terrible position. Still, using the same online databases as before, the checkmate shown in the preceding diagram has been reached more than 100,000 times—so it can happen.

This should give you a sense of how gambits for Black work. There are very few gambits for Black that leave Black in a good position if White knows the best moves to respond. With gambits for Black, if the tricks and traps don't work, you often end up in a worse position than your opponent. Use the QR code at the end of the chapter to explore some other Black gambits that can lead to decent positions for Black even if the traps don't work, such as the Portuguese and Budapest Gambits.

Summary

Gambits are early sacrifices of material that seek to gain some form of advantage. In some cases, dominant spatial control is acquired, while in others, a devastating assault emerges on the enemy king. Gambits can be accepted or declined, however, so you must be prepared to play a "normal" game of chess regardless.

When playing White, gambits can skyrocket your speed of piece development and help you control the central squares. This early lead will usually lead to the regaining of material and potentially strong attacks.

With Black, however, gambits usually carry a far greater risk-to-reward ratio. Moving second in chess is already a slight disadvantage, but when you combine that with an early loss of material, disaster can quickly follow. That's why gambits such as the Englund or Blackburne-Shilling look for knockouts within the first ten moves.

Some gambits are cheap tricks—like the two just mentioned—and are merely meant for fun, like pouring a bit of hot sauce on your meal. Others, such as the Danish Gambit or King's Gambit, are perfectly legitimate long-term tools for your chess opening development.

Follow this QR code to explore gambits for White and Black in more detail.

CHAPTER THIRTEEN

INTERMEDIATE ENDGAMES

This was by far the hardest chapter to write because we have a limited number of pages to convey a huge amount of information. My goal is to convey this information to you efficiently and concisely so you understand as much as possible about different endgame scenarios. That's a challenge because there are entire 400–500 page books that are just about endgames. The goal of this chapter is to introduce different kinds of endgames and give you the tools to better understand them and play for the best result. I'll also be introducing a bunch of terms that can be applied not just to endgames but across all phases of the game.

The first thing to do is define what we mean by "endgame." An endgame is defined, very generally, as a scenario where there aren't many pieces left on the board. Think about it like this: if you were to take your seven pieces (excluding pawns and the king, so two knights, two bishops, two rooks, and the queen) and remove more than half of them, plus a few pawns, you'd be in an endgame. You have fifteen pieces that can be captured

(the king cannot be). If half or more are gone, I'd say that's an endgame.

The next important thing to know is that certain endgames in chess have been solved. The first one we'll look at—king and pawn versus king—has been solved. "Solved" means that with optimal play the result is known. Depending on where the pieces are and whose turn it is, the game should always end in a particular result with best play. Openings and middlegames can be very unpredictable but certain endgames are known to be winning, losing, or a draw—but again, only with best play, which means knowing how to turn a solved winning position into a win.

In these solved endgames, there's no such thing as a better or worse position for one side or the other. These endgames are either winning, drawing, or losing with best play—there aren't many more nuances to it, particularly with the most basic endgame scenarios like king and pawn versus king. The other type of endgames are practical endgames. These are not solved but they are *winnable* rather than certainly winning.

How you apply pressure and use the right techniques will determine whether you can turn winnable into a win. Your opponent may defend correctly and hold the game, but you need to know how to apply the right pressure. Magnus Carlsen, the current world champion, is renowned for his endgame stamina. He frequently will grind players down in five- or six-hour games by posing constant problems to his opponents in winnable endgames and then eventually win.

There are some key terms related to endgames that you'll see throughout this chapter. There are certain factors that determine whether an endgame is winning, drawing, or losing: material, activity, weaknesses, *zugzwang*, domination, and passed pawns. These will all be explored in more detail in this chapter.

King and Pawn Endgames

Let's kick off with a basic example:

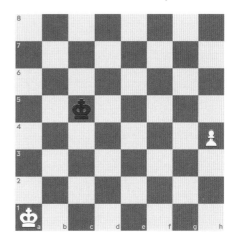

♟ White is trying to get the pawn to the end of the board and promote to a queen. White is four squares away from doing that. Depending on whose move it is, this position has a solved result. If it's White's move, the Black king cannot stop the pawn; White will get a queen and deliver the King and Queen Mate. If it's Black's turn, Black will be able to defend the h8 square one move before White makes a queen. Black will capture the pawn and the game will be a draw.

This is a concept known as the **square**. However, how many squares the pawn is from promotion determines the dimensions of the square, so if the pawn is four squares from promotion then the square would be 4 x 4. In this position, this is the square:

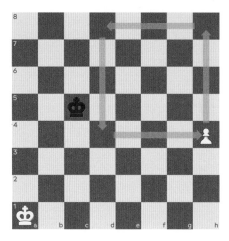

⬆ Black needs to be inside the square to stop White from promoting. So, if it were Black's turn, Black would move into the square and this means the pawn cannot promote before the king captures it. If it were Black's turn in this position . . .

. . . this is the how the race would end. White can technically promote but Black will capture the queen and the game is a draw. ⬇

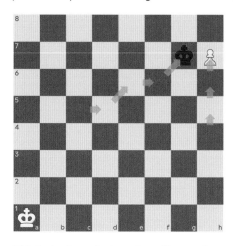

This is the foundation of any king and pawn endgame. In this endgame, the side with the pawn wants to make a queen in order to checkmate and win.

Now let's look at a position where both kings are involved:

✎ This position, with best play, is a draw *no matter whose move it is*. This is a solved endgame. Actually, this endgame is theoretically a draw any time the pawn stands in front of its king, because the enemy king will always be able to stop further progress. Still, Black needs to know the technique here. Black *must* step straight back, then follow White's king. Let's say it's Black's turn and Black moves . . .

⬆ . . . back to d7, after which the White king moves to e5. White is trying to escort the pawn safely to the back rank and promote a queen. Here it's critical Black gets into opposition with the White king . . .

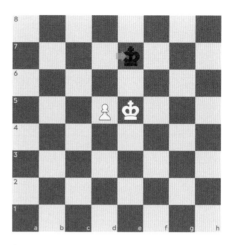

⬆ . . . like this. White cannot move the king forward so will likely play . . .

⬆ . . . pawn to d6, and Black will move back in front of the pawn. This position is almost a repeat of the earlier position, only one rank closer to the end of the board. If Black repeats the same technique, the game will end . . .

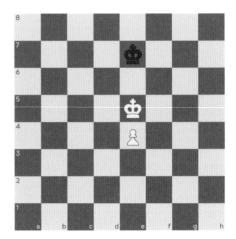

♟ . . . like this. It's Black's turn and therefore stalemate—Black has no legal moves—and Black has therefore secured a draw.

This is something very fundamental you must know about king and pawn endgames—both if you are the player up a pawn or down a pawn. If you're down a pawn, you need to know the technique of blockading the enemy pawn with your own king in order to secure a draw. You also need to know how to win it if you are the player up a pawn. The key is having the king in front of the pawn rather than behind. Let's say we've done that and this is the position:

♙ Is this position winning or a draw for White? Actually, that's a trick question because it depends on whose move it is. If it's White's move, it's a draw because Black will always move into opposition and prevent White from getting the pawn through. However, if it's Black's turn here then they are forced to move out of opposition . . .

♟ . . . at which point the White king moves forward to the opposite side and takes more space. This nuance is tremendously important for converting winning positions into wins. From here, the Black king will have to retreat . . .

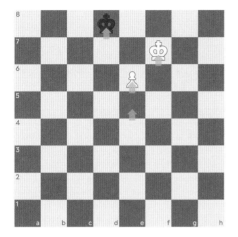

⬆ . . . and we'll end up in a position like this. The White king on f7 escorts the pawn to the end of the board, where the Black king will not be able to capture it because the White king defends. White will make a queen and win.

This is a technique you have to understand. One caveat: this technique only works on files b–g. If the pawn you are trying to promote is on the a or h file (the outside files), the game is a draw. The technique no longer works because your king doesn't have the space to force the opposing king backward:

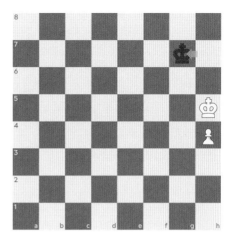

⬆ Here you would need an i file to apply the same technique. But there isn't an additional file, so this would be a draw with best play.

Of course, king and pawn endgames can occur with more than one pawn on the board. Let's look at a more complex position:

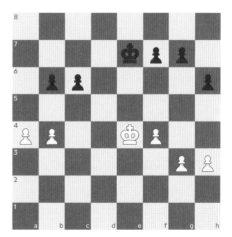

⬆ For an endgame to be winning, there needs to be some kind of imbalance. Here the material is equal. Other factors we need to think about are king activity, weaknesses, and one thing that gives White a particular advantage here—an outside passed pawn (a pawn on an outside file that can't be captured by any enemy pawns). Here White should play . . .

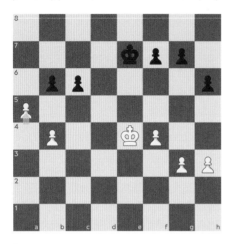

↟ . . . pawn to a5. Black will capture and White will recapture, giving us . . .

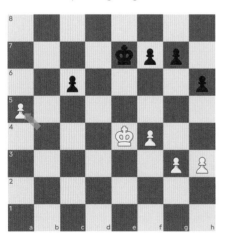

↦ . . . this position. Now White has an outside passed pawn that is threatening to become a queen. Black now has to run their king all the way over to capture the pawn, by which time White . . .

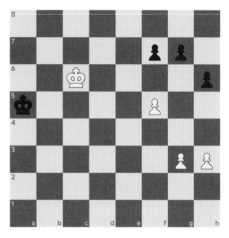

↟ . . . will capture Black's c6 pawn. White's king is now much closer to the pawns on the other side of the board, and can capture all the Black pawns and escort one of the White pawns through to the back rank to promote.

Here White has used the threat of an outside passed pawn as a decoy to transform the position into a winning endgame. In king and pawn endgames, king activity is extremely important. So too is creating a passed pawn—ideally one on the far edge of the board—that can either run through and become a queen or at least take the opposing king away from the action.

Knight Endgames

Now let's add some more pieces to the end-game board, starting with knights:

♟ . . . this is a completely winning endgame for Black. Black will again use the outside passed pawn as a constant threat—a decoy that drags either White's king or knight over to stop it from promoting—allowing Black to capture White's pawns and create another passed pawn on the f or g file. This is something we'd call "two weaknesses," where one side cannot both protect their own pawns and prevent an enemy pawn from promoting. The two weaknesses for White in this case are the Black pawn on a5 and their own pawns; White has to choose whether to stop Black's a pawn promotion or keep their king and/or knight protecting White's own pawns from being captured by Black's king.

♟ This position is a draw. Material is exactly equal, both players have a pawn cluster, and both have active kings. This will end in a draw by trading off all the pieces or even just trading off the pawns—king and knight cannot checkmate a king, as we know, so it will automatically be a draw when all the pawns fall off the board here. Even if one of Black's pawns were all the way on the other side of the board, as long as the White king remains in the square then the pawn should never be able to promote. But if Black has both their pawns in the above position and another outside passed pawn . . .

Another example of this "two weaknesses" concept comes from a famous game played between Michael Adams and Jonathan Speelman in 1995:

🨅 This is the endgame. Despite White having an extra pawn, this should be a draw. However, a few more moves were played and White managed to pick up another of Black's pawns after delivering a knight fork . . .

🨇 . . . which allowed the knight to capture one of Black's pawns. White then used their pawns as decoys to end up . . .

🨅 . . . in this position. White is now only up one pawn, and if Black is able to sacrifice their knight for White's pawn (i.e., capture the pawn with the knight, even if it means losing the knight), it will be a draw by insufficient checkmating material. The end result was White trapping Black's knight, forcing the knights to trade and White finding themselves in a winning king and pawn versus king endgame. You can see the full endgame played out by using the QR code at the end of the chapter.

Knight vs. Bishop Endgames

The key thing when talking about knight versus bishop endgames is that bishops move much faster around the board and there are times when a bishop can dominate a knight. Take this position:

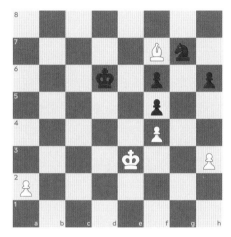

♙ This is from a game between Aloyzas Kveinys and Krzysztof Ejsmont in 2006. Material is equal here but White has an outside passed pawn and the Black knight at the moment cannot move at all. Anywhere it moves, it would be captured by one of White's pieces. Again, White uses the outside passed pawn as a decoy, forcing Black's king to run over and capture it.

Now this is a completely winning endgame for White. The Black knight still cannot move, and White's king will march over, gobble up Black's pieces, and escort one of their pawns to the back rank, where it will promote. Black

resigned in this position before any of that could happen. ⬇

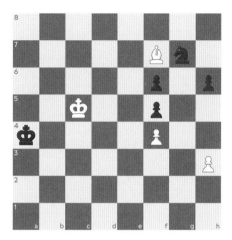

That is an example of how a bishop can dominate a knight. That isn't to say a knight can't dominate a bishop in certain situations. Look at this position:

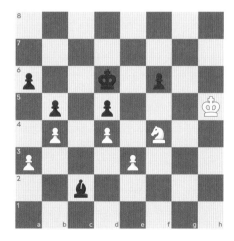

♙ Here Black's bishop is ineffective because every White pawn is on a dark square. When you're playing against a bishop in the endgame, try to keep your pawns on the opposite color complex of that bishop. White's knight is more powerful in this game.

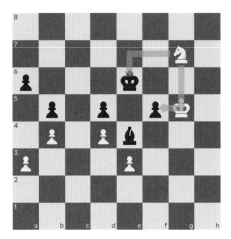

⬆ White will try to get to a position like this, where White's knight and king team up to capture one of Black's pawns, converting this into a winning endgame for White. Notice how all six of White's remaining pieces are on dark squares in this position, making Black's light-squared bishop completely useless.

Knights can therefore theoretically be better in an endgame than bishops, though generally speaking, bishops are better pieces (we'll look at this more in Chapter Fifteen).

Bishop Endgames

Bishop endgames are unique. The first type of bishop endgame I want to look at is opposite-colored bishop endgames. Take this position:

⬆ This position is a draw no matter what. In opposite-colored bishop endgames, a one-pawn advantage—specifically one pawn versus zero—doesn't mean you're going to win the game. This is because, as with the knight, Black's light-squared bishop can sacrifice itself for White's remaining pawn when it crosses into its path. That will be a draw because a king and bishop cannot checkmate a king. Because White has a dark-squared bishop, White cannot block or attack the opposing light-squared bishop and help the pawn escape its laser beam.

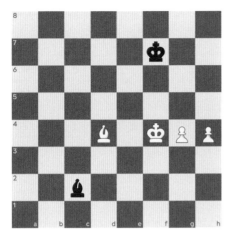

♟ Even wilder, if White had another pawn, it should still be a draw. With the right defense, there should be no way for White to get a pawn through for promotion. Between Black's bishop and king, they should be able to blockade or capture the pawns and simplify down to a drawn endgame by insufficient checkmating material.

🡒 However, if we consider a position where one of White's pawns is on the other side of the board, this is winning for White. Black's bishop and king will find it impossible to stop both pawns advancing simultaneously.

So, while scattered pawns can be a real weakness in middlegames, in endgames they can be a gem. They divide the attention of the opposing pieces and give the opponent too much to worry about. This is true in opposite-colored bishop endgames but also in bishop endgames of the same color.

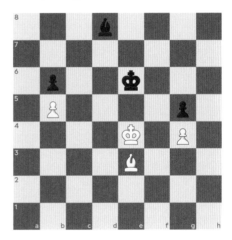

♟ In this position, material is equal and both sides have a dark-squared bishop. As we learned earlier, if a player has a certain-colored bishop they'll want to put their pawns on the opposite color. White is winning in this position because Black's bishop is completely stuck protecting both the Black pawns—if it moves anywhere, it will stop defending one of the pawns and White will be able to capture it with their own bishop. Likewise, if Black's king moves in either direction, White's king will run in the other direction and win whichever pawn it can, ultimately creating a passed pawn that it can escort to the back rank and promote.

In the previous position, Black is in something known as *zugzwang*, which is a situation in chess where a player has to move (because it's their turn) but any move they make will worsen their position and likely lead to defeat.

In same-colored bishop endgames, king activity and keeping your pawns on the opposite color to your opponent's bishop can make all the difference. Look at this position from a game between Magnus Carlsen and Alireza Firouzja in 2021:

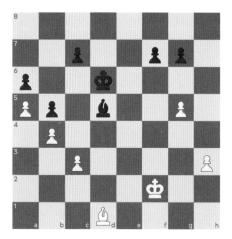

↑ Carlsen has the White pieces and this is the position after thirty moves. Material is equal and bishops are the same color—most players would shake hands here and head off for something to eat. But over the next ten moves . . .

. . . Carlsen maneuvers all his pawns to dark squares—safe from Black's light-squared bishop—and has also frozen (meaning they cannot move forward) all of Firouzja's pawns on light squares . . . ↓

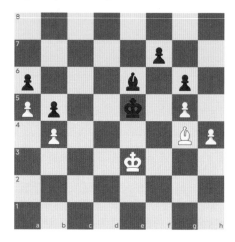

. . . After a few more moves have been played, Carlsen actually sacrifices a pawn for a more active king. White's king now threatens to run over to Black's a and b pawns and win them. ↓

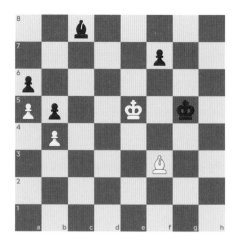

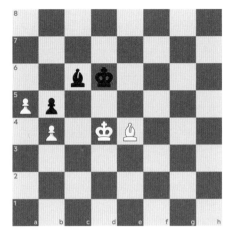

⬆ The final position from this game looked like this. Firouzja resigned here. White has a passed pawn and will slowly find a way to escort it to promotion. Carlsen won an endgame of complete symmetry here by forcing his opponent into difficult decisions every move and by working a situation where his light-squared bishop threatened his opponent's pawns—stuck on light squares—while his own pawns were safe on the dark squares. You can see the full endgame played out by using the QR code at the end of the chapter.

Rook Endgames

In rook endgames, if one player has a pawn then the objective will again be to push the pawn down the board with the aim of promoting it to a queen. Remember that king and rook versus king is winning—we looked at the technique for this checkmate earlier in the book (pages 57–60). Let's look at an example where both players have a rook, though:

⬆ White is up a pawn but there is another reason this is winning for White. White's rook is **cutting off** the Black king. The Black king cannot cross the c file because White has a rook there. Black's king is now denied access to 52 of the 64 squares on the board because of where White's rook is positioned. This means Black's king will never be able to come across and help the Black rook as White . . .

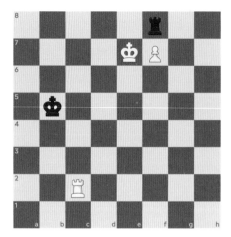

♟ . . . escorts their pawn to the end of the board with their king. Black will end up losing their rook here and White will eventually deliver checkmate with their king and rook (and/or their new queen, if Black doesn't stop the pawn promoting).

That, in a nutshell, is what the attacking side wants in rook endgames: to cut off the enemy king on the other side of the board with their rook and use their king to escort a pawn to promotion. Rooks can cut off a king from the game the way bishops and knights cannot. Rooks can also be very effective when positioned behind the pawn that you are trying to promote. It's important to show that rook and pawn versus rook isn't automatically winning, however:

♟ This is known as the Philidor Position, which is more of a technique than a position in the traditional sense. This position is a draw if Black plays the move . . .

♟ . . . rook a6. Black cuts off White's king and if the pawn goes forward . . .

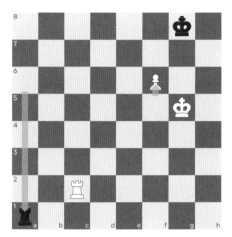

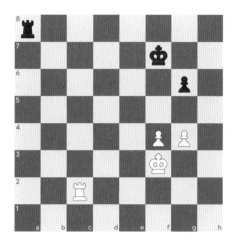

🔼 . . . the rook drops down to the back rank and will be able to give constant checks both horizontally and vertically, meaning White will never make any progress. The game will therefore be a draw because Black will constantly be able to check White's king, so it will end up a draw by repetition or by agreement. It's important to know this is a theoretical endgame; that is, it's solved. You need to know this defensive technique; otherwise you'll likely lose this position when it should be a draw.

Another important thing to note is that top players would consider a position like this one a draw:

🔼 No grandmaster would try to win this position despite White having an extra pawn. That's because of the Philidor technique. It also wouldn't matter if White had three pawns and Black had two—they'd still shake hands and go grab a drink (of juice, kids). However, a pawn on the other side . . .

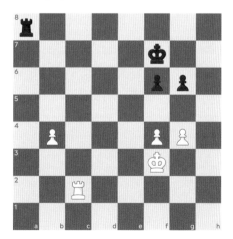

🔼 . . . is a very different story. This is three pawns versus two, but one is on the other side of the board. If White positions their rook behind the b pawn, Black is very unlikely to be able to stop the pawn promotion while also protecting their f and g pawns from White's king—Black's king is needed to both stop the b pawn promoting and defend the f and g pawns from White's king. The b pawn will again be a decoy . . .

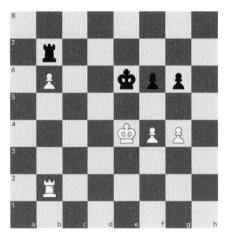

♟ . . . that will need constant monitoring from Black's pieces. Black is unable to deal with the threat of the advancing pawn and the White king infiltrating and grabbing the other pawns.

Pawns on the same side of the board in rook endgames will likely be a draw. Scattered pawns again offer an opportunity to win, as we've seen in other types of endgames. Rook endgames are some of the most complicated in chess.

Queen Endgames

Last but not least, let's look at endgames with the queen. We'll start with queen versus pawn, which is a very important endgame to understand. Queen versus one pawn is a solved endgame and should always be winning for the player with the queen. Let's start with the most fundamental example so we can understand the theory here:

♟ White has a queen. Black wants to escort their pawn to d1 and make a queen of their own. White needs to capture the pawn but to do so they need to separate the Black king from defense of the pawn. The technique for doing this is to get the queen . . .

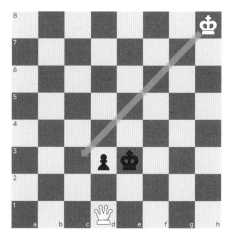 ... in front of the pawn. Black now cannot move their king any closer and so cannot break through and promote the pawn. White will then bring their own king ...

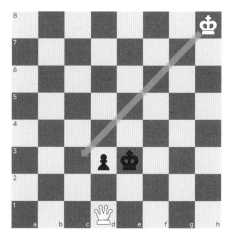 ... all the way down the board, to capture the pawn and use the King and Queen Mate technique we looked at in the early chapters (see pages 54–57) to win the game.

But what happens if the position is trickier?

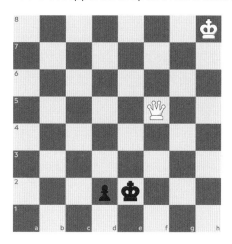

 Is this position still winning for White? Black is one square away from making a queen of their own, protected by their king. It is actually still winning for White, but only if the pawn is on one of the b, d, e, or g files. The reason for this is that the technique required to separate the king from the pawn doesn't work if the pawn is an a, c, f, or h pawn.

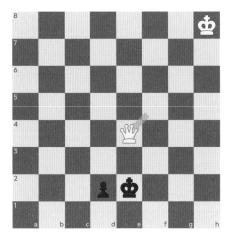

🡑 The technique begins with check, with the White queen moving to e4. Let's say Black plays king to f2, at which point we play . . .

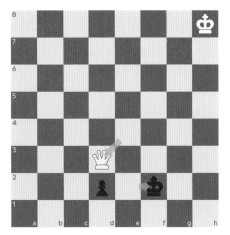

🡑 . . . queen to d3, threatening to capture the pawn and stopping it from promoting.

🡑 Black then plays king to e1, protecting the pawn, and we play the check needed in this position—queen to e3. This forces the king to d1—if king f1, White captures the pawn—where it stops its own pawn from promoting . . .

🡑 . . . and again the key is then to bring your king across the board and eventually capture the pawn with your king and queen together—the queen will capture, protected by the king.

The reason why this is a draw on the a and h files is that White can either force a stalemate or an endless loop of moves with no progress:

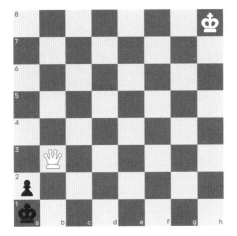

⬆ Here White has done the same thing of forcing the Black king in front of its own pawn. Under normal circumstances, you'd start by bringing the king over to where the other pieces are. But if White moves their king in this situation, it's stalemate—Black has no legal moves. So instead White has to move their queen, which means Black can move their king again, and so on until both players give up and agree to a draw.

It's even more fascinating if it's a pawn on the c or f file:

⬆ White seems to have done everything right and found the check they wanted, which should force the Black king in front of their own pawn. But instead, the Black king . . .

⬆ . . . will go to the corner of the board, abandoning the c pawn to die. But if White captures the pawn, it's stalemate. So, White did everything right but failed because of the mysteries of board geometry!

Queen versus pawn is a theoretical endgame, which means computers have proven the same result should always be reached and best play will always result in either a draw or win, depending on which pawn file the pawn occupies. But other queen endgames are much more complicated. Generally, the king plays less of a role in endgames involving queens, particularly since leaving your king out in the open can lead to problems when the opponent still has a queen. This is from the eleventh round of the 1960 World Championship game between Mikhail Tal and Mikhail Botvinnik:

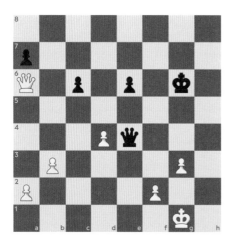

♟ In queen and pawn endgames, the person with more pawns is usually playing for a win. But something you have to be careful of in queen endgames is **perpetual check**, which is when a king is forced into an unavoidable series of checks, often resulting in a draw by repetition. Tal, playing White, has two extra pawns in this position . . .

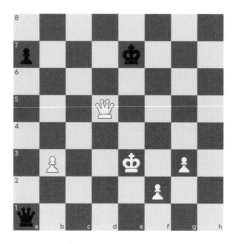

♟ . . . and he got the position down to this endgame. If this were a rook endgame (i.e., if White and Black had rooks instead of queens) it would be a certain win for White. But because Black has a queen, Tal has to find a place to "hide" his king where it won't be harassed with endless checks. Botvinnik eventually resigned because White did an effective job of protecting the king from constant checks, but perpetual check is something you need to be aware of—even if you are clearly winning, if your opponent has a queen they may be able to check your king forever and force a draw if your king isn't somewhere safe. Make sure your king is protected at all times in queen endgames. As always, the full endgame can be seen by following the QR code on the following page.

Summary

The endgame is all about combining theoretical positions—meaning those that are solved with best play—with practical ones, where the best plans depend entirely on the situation on the board. The evaluation and result of an endgame—meaning whether it is won, drawn, or lost—is determined by a combination of material imbalance, piece activity, and weaknesses for both White and Black.

Pawn endgames are the backbone of all endgames. At the end of the day, you will either promote successfully to a queen and win the game or not. We discussed both the roles of the pawns and kings and how to win or draw from a certain position. Understanding whether a pawn endgame is winning or not will allow you to simplify down from a position with more pieces on the board.

In most cases, a bishop is better than a knight in the endgame because it's quicker around the board and because it can potentially restrict the movement of a knight. When it comes to pawns, equality is preferred, but being down one pawn does not mean defeat since there is an option to sacrifice your piece for the remaining pawn. Outside passed pawns—those on the a and h files—are the greatest assets in this case, along with the centralization and activity of the kings. Opposite-colored bishop endgames are very often drawable, even when down two pawns. Keep that in mind when defending an unpleasant position!

Rook endgames are some of the most complex in chess—there are manuals written for them that are thousands of pages long. Remember the objective: promoting a pawn and often checkmating with king and rook versus king. The Philidor Position is a defensive technique to restrain a player from advancing, relying on constant checks to neutralize progress.

In queen endgames, it is important to learn how to stop a "runaway pawn." The simplest way is to stand on the promotion square, but you must learn the winning technique if that is not possible. When each side has a queen, things are different. The power of a queen renders material imbalance obsolete compared to other endgames. The objective here is still promotion of a pawn, but a queen can patrol multiple sides of the board and rely on the threat of a perpetual check to save the game.

Follow this QR code to explore some of the endgame concepts covered in this chapter.

CHAPTER FOURTEEN
INTERMEDIATE TACTICS

In Chapter Seven, we looked at the fundamentals of piece interactions and an introduction to tactics. A lot of that was based on an immediate tactical opportunity or at most a possible tactic one or two moves into the future. Those sequences usually resulted in you winning material or checkmating the opponent. As an intermediate player, you must start adding other important concepts and techniques to your tactical play as you face increasingly adept opponents.

The most important thing to know as you move into intermediate play is that "tactics" as an intermediate or advanced player are all about pattern recognition. This might be an extreme analogy that makes you laugh, but we are all born as babies. None of us can speak, walk, or solve checkmates in two or three as a baby. The best chess players in the world have simply trained and seen certain types of positions literally tens of thousands of times. Their brains no longer have to think; they do not need to analyze or evaluate certain positions or configurations but instead simply recognize certain patterns that are ripe for winning tactics.

To use my boxing analogy again, I have a habit of blinking every time a punch comes anywhere near me—even when we're drilling in slow motion. This means I need to develop muscle memory to the point that my opponent can throw five punches at me and I don't blink even once. That's not something you're born with but rather something that needs to be trained. In chess, pattern recognition is everything and that comes from practicing with a physical board or online. You have to practice tactics over and over so that when opportunities present themselves in a game, you recognize them instinctively.

The other important thing to know as you move into intermediate play concerns the mindset you need to have—not just for spotting and solving tactics but for any position in a chess game where it's your move—which we call CCA. This stands for **checks, captures, attacks**. That is your list of things to look for in any *position*, for both yourself and your opponent. All of those things are forcing moves, moves that force your opponent into responding in a way that you can predict and therefore calculate ahead. Moves that aren't forcing might allow your opponent a choice of something like thirty responses, depending on the position and how many pieces are on the board. You can't predict them all and therefore can't plan how you'll continue your attack. If you play a forcing move, your opponent's options will be significantly reduced and that allows you to calculate what might happen next. We're going to look at some examples with two- or three-move sequences, some of which will be checkmating attacks, and others that will be about removing the guard, *zwischenzug* (an in-between move), discovered attacks, deflections, attractions, or sacrifices.

Beginning to Use CCA

Let's begin with this position:

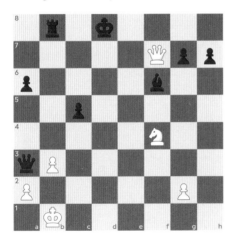

⬆ Black has a four-point material advantage and actually, if it were Black's move, Black would have checkmate by playing queen to b2. However, it's White's move and White is winning in this position because White has checkmate in two.

But how? What does that even mean? If you look at the position, White has a lot of

different checks. Based on our CCA checklist (checks, captures, attacks), White has many potential checks they could play. How do you evaluate the different checks to find the one that leads to checkmate in two? When we say "checkmate in two," we are saying there is an unavoidable checkmate for White if they find the correct two moves.

The first check you should consider is the one that allows for the fewest responses from your opponent. There are a lot of queen checks for White in this position—queen to f8, queen to g8, queen to d5, queen to d7, or queen to e8 (the last two lose the queen)—but every one of the safe checks allows your opponent a choice of at least two moves in response.

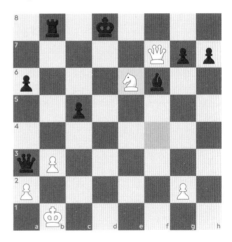

⬆ Instead of playing a queen check, the move knight to e6 leaves Black with only one legal move, which is . . .

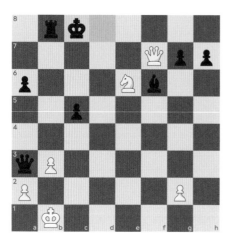

♟ . . . king to c8, and now White has the move . . .

Looking for checks is how you begin incorporating the CCA checklist into your attacking play. When you have a choice of multiple checks, evaluate each one and prioritize checks that allow your opponent the fewest responses. That doesn't mean that the most forcing check is necessarily the winning move, but it's the best place to start your calculations. If you calculate that the most forcing check doesn't get you anywhere, then move on to analyzing other checks you might have in the position. It isn't just about looking for checks; it's about finding all the checks, analyzing them in turn, and choosing the one that leads to the best continuation of the position.

CCA: The Next Level

Let's look at another position:

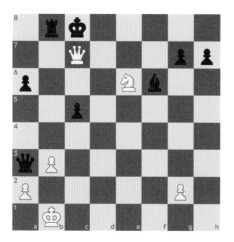

♟ . . . queen to c7, which is checkmate. The queen attacks the Black king and is defended from capture by the White knight on e6. White has to find that right now, too, otherwise Black has checkmate on the next move by playing queen to b2—Black's queen would be protected by the bishop on f6.

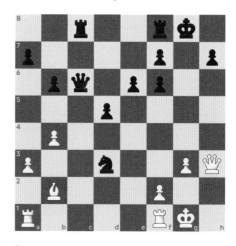

♟ Here the material situation is less dire than we saw in the previous example, but Black is still up three pawns and White's bishop is under attack from Black's knight.

Maybe if you were playing this game with the White pieces and your opponent just moved the knight to d3 to attack your bishop, your instinct would be to move the bishop so it isn't captured. That seems the logical thing to do. But we should apply the CCA checklist here, too—even when one of our pieces is under attack. The first thing you have to look for—not necessarily play, but look for and consider—is a check. In this position, there's a concept I like to call **danger levels**, which means potentially ignoring an opponent's threat by making one of your own that is equal or exceeding in danger.

So here, using the CCA checklist and this concept of danger levels, instead of saving our bishop from the knight's attack we have another option:

⬆ What's worth more than a bishop? A king. If we play queen to g4 check, our bishop is still under attack but Black can't capture it because they have to protect their king. Black has one legal move . . .

⬆ . . . which is king to h8. Only now do we move our bishop, not just to save it from the knight attack . . .

⬆ . . . but also to deliver checkmate on f6. This is another example of why you need to think about the CCA checklist before rushing into moves. Without looking for checks, we might have just moved the bishop to safety and the game would have continued; now, because we used the checklist, we managed to win the game.

CCA: Checkmate in Three

We've looked at two examples of checkmate in two. Now let's add another layer by looking at checkmate in three:

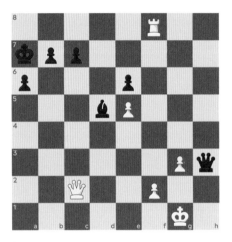

⬆ Black is once again threatening mate on White (queen to g2 or h1 is checkmate), but it's White's move. Given that Black will checkmate White if given the opportunity, all of White's moves need to be checks to avoid losing. White has two possible checks in this position: rook to a8, which will simply result in losing the rook, and queen to c5. Only one of these moves makes sense.

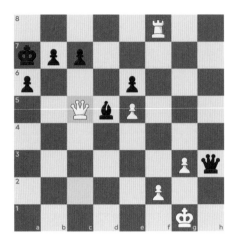

⬆ White plays queen to c5. In response, Black has only one legal move . . .

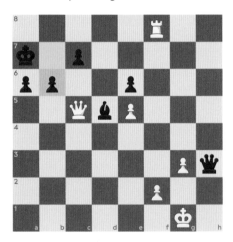

⬆ . . . which is blocking with the king with a pawn on b6. White needs to continue playing checks; otherwise Black will checkmate White. So White needs to play . . .

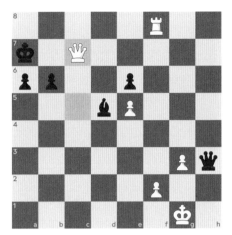

⬆ . . . queen takes pawn on c7 check. A move ago this wouldn't have been check and Black would have checkmated White. It's not over, though. Again, Black has only one legal move . . .

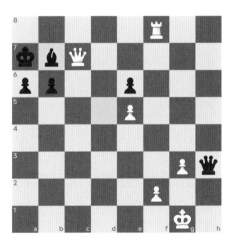

⬆ . . . which is bishop to b7, blocking the queen's attack. Now it's checkmate in one. Can you see it? White plays . . .

. . . queen to b8 checkmate. The queen is defended by the rook and the Black king has nowhere safe to run. ⬇

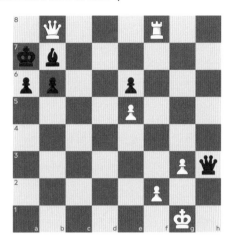

The more you practice checkmate puzzles and drills, the better you will become at identifying opportunities to checkmate. The point is not to be trying to force checkmates all the time by playing as many checks as possible; rather, you will improve your pattern recognition and develop better instincts for checkmating attacks. This is just as important from a defensive standpoint as it is from an attacking standpoint. Developing these pattern recognition skills will help you spot danger in your own position as much as weaknesses in your opponent's.

CCA: Winning Material

Checkmating is obviously the ultimate goal in chess but it's important to look at some positions where the CCA checklist might not necessarily lead to instant wins. Take this position:

♟ Black is up one point of material but overall the position is relatively balanced. Both sides have five pawns and a bishop, while Black has two knights and a rook versus two rooks for White. Let's think about our CCA checklist. White has one check in this position—capturing Black's pawn on f7 with the bishop, which will result in losing a bishop for a pawn. So, we can reject that. Instead we move on to the next aspect of the checklist, which is captures. White has the same capture option of the pawn on f7, which we've already determined would be a bad move and result in losing the bishop. The other capture White has is . . .

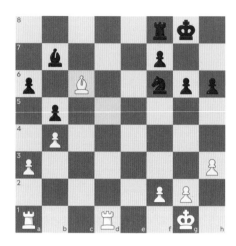

♟ . . . bishop takes the knight on c6, after which Black will . . .

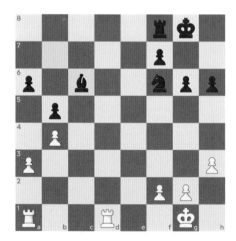

♟ . . . recapture with their own bishop. Normally that's just a fair trade; a bishop and knight are both worth three points, so nobody is better or worse after the exchange. But White has a follow-up move that does win material, using something we learned in

Chapter Eight. What if I told you there's a fork here? When looking at a position, we should be looking for weaknesses—pieces that aren't defended by any other pieces. Here White can play . . .

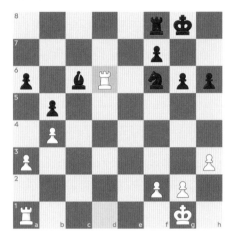

♟ . . . rook d6. This forks—attacks—both Black's bishop and knight and Black has no way to defend them both. We got here by using the CCA checklist. We looked at checks and found there weren't any useful ones. Next we looked at captures and calculated that after the pieces were traded, we'd have a fork that would win us more material. Rook to d6 is an attack, the third part of the checklist. This doesn't win the game immediately, but we are going to win one of Black's pieces and have a very decisive advantage in the endgame.

CCA is designed to make you analyze every single position you find yourself in during a chess game. It isn't just for checkmates; it's for making decisions throughout an entire game. Combined with some of the lessons we

explored earlier about weaknesses, the CCA checklist will help you think more logically in different situations and hopefully strike decisive blows on your opponent's position.

Removing the Defender

Often in chess, you'll see opportunities to win material or deliver checkmate that aren't immediately possible because the opponent has a piece defending the situation. "Removing the defender" means forcibly removing—either by capturing or attacking—an enemy piece that is defending another enemy piece, or preventing you from delivering checkmate.

♟ Look at this position and think about the CCA checklist: checks, captures, attacks. If we're playing White, we have one check; queen takes pawn on h7. Our queen forms a battery with our bishop on c2, so at first glance it might look like checkmate, except the Black knight is defending the pawn and would simply capture the White queen. Instead of dismissing this potential checkmate, in this situation you should be thinking about ways to get rid of the knight. How do we do that?

♟ We play pawn to g5. This attacks the Black knight and if Black moves it, White can now deliver checkmate on h7. In this position, Black, instead of moving the knight, has to block White's potential checkmate by playing pawn to g6. That will prevent White's checkmate, but also will mean Black losing the knight when White captures it with their pawn on the next move.

This is what it means to remove the defender. You can remove the defender of a square or you can remove the defender of a piece. Again, we found this tactic by using the CCA checklist. We found a check that would have been fatal and looked for a way to make the check happen by playing an attack on the defender.

Zwischenzug

A *zwischenzug* is a tactic where, before you play the correct move, you play an "in-between" move that is usually very forcing. This might be because you can capture extra material with your in-between move or because you're stopping something bad happening to your own pieces. Let's look at an example:

♟ Here Black just captured a pawn in the center with the knight. If we were playing White, normally we would just capture the knight with our pawn on c3, which is a winning trade for White. But if you do that, Black will play bishop takes bishop on b5 and it will end up an even trade. So, prior to taking the knight on d4 we can play a *zwischenzug* . . .

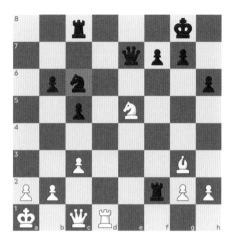

♟ . . . bishop takes d7 check. It's an in-between move, a forcing move that Black must respond to (it's check). When Black captures our bishop, then we take their knight on d4 and we're up material. If a move isn't very forcing (usually a check or otherwise an attack on a powerful piece like the queen or rook) then it wouldn't be an in-between move. A *zwischenzug* is a move that the opponent must respond to, which we play before we play the expected move on our next turn.

A *zwischenzug* doesn't always have to be a check. Take the position shown next:

♙ After a series of exchanges, White has a choice of which piece to capture next. We can either capture the rook on f2 with our bishop or capture the knight on c6 with our own knight. One of these is the expected move, and one is an in-between move. A free rook would generally seem better than a fair exchange of knights, but in this case the rook isn't going anywhere if we capture the knight . . .

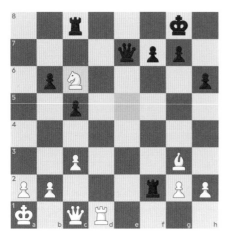

⬆ . . . with our knight. Our knight now attacks Black's queen. If it didn't, Black would be able to move their f2 rook to safety, but instead Black has to capture our knight with their c8 rook in order to protect their queen. White can then play the expected move—capturing the rook on f2 with the bishop—on their next turn and be up a significant amount of material.

Zwischenzugs, or in-between moves, are very important tactics to add to your pattern recognition toolbox because they often can be the difference between a winning tactical skirmish and an equal or even losing one.

Discovered Attacks

We touched on discoveries earlier but it's worth looking at a couple of examples with our CCA checklist in mind. A discovered attack is when one of your pieces creates danger on an enemy piece because another of your pieces moves out of the way. The most effective type of discovered attack is

when you create a threat with two pieces at the same time—the piece you are moving creates a threat *and* the piece behind it creates a different threat. Take this position:

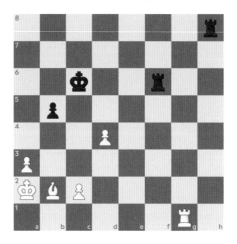

⬆ If White uses the CCA checklist, they should find the move . . .

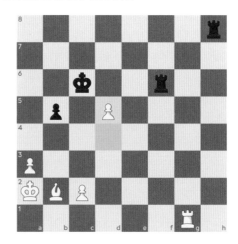

⬆ . . . pawn to d5, which is White's only check in this position. Because it's check, Black has to deal with the pawn attacking the

Black king. But moving the pawn has created another attack on the Black position—White's bishop now attacks Black's rook and, because Black has to deal with the check, White can capture the rook on their next turn.

Let's look at another example:

🡙 There is a powerful potential discovered attack here. This is a position that comes from the French Defense, Milner-Barry Gambit, which sets up a trap on the next move. White plays . . .

🡙 . . . bishop b5 check. This is a discovered attack on Black's queen by White's queen. Black has to deal with the check and on White's next turn they can capture Black's queen, putting them into a strong winning position.

Remember that this discovered attack works because the bishop is delivering check. If the bishop simply moved and it wasn't check, Black would be free to capture the White queen and it would simply be an even trade.

Sacrifices, Deflection, and Attraction

Here is another position, this time involving a sacrifice—which in chess means giving up material with the aim of getting tactical or positional compensation: 🡙

This position comes from the Sicilian Defense. Here Black . . .

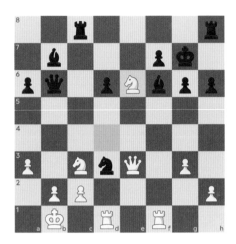

♟ ... plays the move knight takes bishop on d3. White can recapture the knight in three different ways—the pawn, the queen, and the rook can all take the knight and it will be an even trade for the bishop White lost. All of those moves are wrong, though. If you thought about capturing the knight, you haven't been paying attention. Be honest, did I catch you? Don't just snap-capture the knight. Think through your CCA checklist of checks, captures, and attacks. If you carefully analyze all checks in this position, you should find the incredible move . . .

♟ ... White knight takes e6 (knight to f5 also works), which is a check. Not only have you not recaptured White's knight, but you're about to lose your knight for a pawn. You sacrifice your knight because of a devastating discovered attack. The queens now see each other. Black would love to capture White's queen, except it's check so Black has to deal with that. On White's next move, they'll be able to capture Black's queen for free.

If you don't use the CCA checklist, you'll never find knight to e6. You'll simply respond to everything your opponent does without looking for and finding these tactical patterns.

Another useful tactic in your toolbox is something called **deflection**, which is when you remove an opposing piece from defending something else or preventing checkmate by "deflecting" it away.

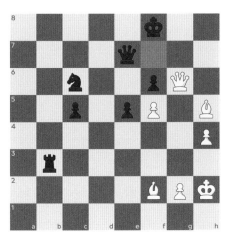

↑ In this position, White has a queen and bishop battery aimed at the f7 square. Only Black's queen is preventing checkmate. So here White's best move is . . .

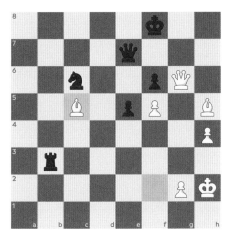

✦ . . . bishop takes c5. This ends the game. Our dark-squared bishop attacks Black's queen; in fact, it's actually a pin, meaning Black cannot move the queen at all except to capture our dark-squared bishop. Except that, when Black does so, the Black queen no longer guards the f7 square . . .

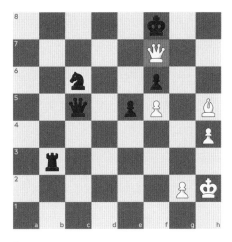

↑ . . . and now the White queen delivers checkmate. We've deflected the Black queen away with a forcing move and won the game.

A similar tactic is something called **attraction**, which is similar to deflection except that you are sacrificing a piece to attract the enemy piece into a worse position. An example of this can be seen in this position:

⬆ Here White has their queen, rook, and knight close to the Black king and is posing lots of danger. Still, White needs to find a way to win the game. The most beautiful next step for White is the move . . .

⬆ . . . rook to h8. This is a sacrifice of a rook. The bishop cannot capture the rook because it's pinned to the king by White's queen, so Black has only one move, which is . . .

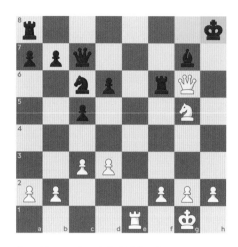

⬆ . . . king takes h8. White has "attracted" the king into the corner and now ends the game with the move . . .

⬆ . . . queen to h7, which is checkmate.

Summary

When playing chess, you should constantly be thinking about CCA: checks, captures, and attacks. This will train your brain into scanning for the most forcing moves in the position for both yourself and your opponent, which will help prevent tactical mistakes and help you capitalize on opportunities. It's important to be able to successfully calculate multiple moves ahead by limiting your opponent's responses due to the forcing nature of your moves.

Removing the defender is a crucial tactic. It attacks an opposing piece which otherwise prevents us from winning material or delivering checkmate, and often the opponent will have to sacrifice the defender to avoid more damage to their position. Always look for opportunities to chase away opposing pieces that are the only thing defending another piece or square.

A *zwischenzug* is an insertion of a forcing move—often a check or a capture—prior to playing a natural move in order to secure some sort of gain. Finding a correct *zwischenzug* requires keen situational awareness.

Discoveries showcase your ability to see how three or four pieces interact at the same time when just one piece gets moved. That is a massive sign of chess understanding! The best situation is one where you create two threats at once.

Sacrifices are deliberate losses of material that intend to cash out at a later moment. Remember how we covered gambits in Chapter Twelve? Think of sacrifices as the gambits of the middlegame—you may sacrifice a knight (3 points) for a pawn (1 point), but in return you shred your opponent's king position and begin a strong attack. Your investment may pay off in the future or fail—that's the beauty of chess!

The tactics of deflection and attraction both require the "baiting" of an enemy piece to a certain location, setting up a powerful and devastating counter.

You do not need to remember all the tactical patterns we covered by name, but it may greatly help you as you try to learn all of the patterns on the board. The only way to genuinely get better at every tactical concept covered in this chapter is to solve chess puzzles—and I don't mean 10, 50, or 100 puzzles—I mean 1,000 puzzles or more!

 Follow this QR code to review some of the tactics we've explored in this chapter.

CHAPTER FIFTEEN

INTERMEDIATE STRATEGY

Congratulations—you made it to the end. I hope you are enjoying the book! This chapter will be the culmination of everything you've learned so far—we will study intermediate strategy in a unique, refreshing way that I have used with students for years. Here we go—the final boss! To advance our understanding of chess strategy, we're going to delve deeper into every piece on the board. We're going to take a closer look at the thought processes needed at different stages of the game and concerning different pieces to really lay the groundwork for taking your chess to the next level. This chapter should help strengthen the foundations we've built throughout this book but remember: every chess player will reach a stage where they have to go off and independently study in order to keep improving. That might mean other books, YouTube content, drilling online puzzles, and/or using a chess engine to analyze your games and review mistakes. Chess is a beautiful game—there are always new things to learn and you can always improve.

Pawns

Let's start with the humble pawn, worth only a single point and seemingly the least important piece on the board. Pawns provide the structure to any position—as we talked about earlier, they are like a fence. We call this concept **pawn structure**. Almost all positions in chess (until there are hardly any or no pawns left on the board) will have some kind of pawn structure. Most openings you play with either White or Black will have some kind of optimal pawn structure associated with them, and understanding those ideal pawn structures will help you mold middlegame plans and find key attacks.

Something else associated with pawn structure is a concept known as **pawn breaks**. A pawn break is a spot in a position where a pawn is pushed forward in the hope that a trade will occur that benefits your position. Usually it will be advantageous to your position because it opens up attacking lines for your pieces or allows one of your major pieces to move to a more active square.

Let's begin by looking at a particular pawn structure:

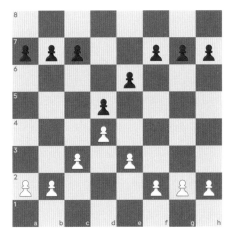

↑ I know this looks bizarre without any of the other pieces. You might recognize how the pawns are positioned here: this is actually the London System pawn structure. The pyramid of White pawns offers good protection for this position, and the e5 square will be good for planting a knight on in the future. An ideal pawn break for Black in this position is to play c5, giving White a choice of whether to capture or not. If White captures, they'll be losing their central pawn and Black may recapture with a knight or bishop and therefore have developed a piece to an advantageous square.

The London pawn structure means it's typically a closed position. We looked at closed versus open positions earlier—the more pawns on a chessboard, the more closed the position. For White, the pawn breaks in this structure would be pushing either the c or e pawn, depending on which pawn is properly supported by one of your pieces (i.e., your knights, bishops, rooks, or queen).

Let's look at a different pawn structure:

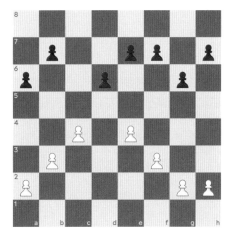

↑ This is a pawn structure from the Maróczy Bind of the Sicilian Defense. Another thing I want to introduce here is a concept called **pawn complexes.** What does that mean? Well, right now White has six out of seven pawns on light squares; that means that White is strong on the light squares because they have lots of them occupied and defended by pawns. White's dark squares, on the other hand, could potentially be like Swiss cheese, leaving holes that Black pieces can get through.

If you have a bunch of pawns on light squares, it might be advantageous to trade off your light-squared bishop for one of your opponent's stronger pieces because your light squares are already reinforced, and the mobility of your light-squared bishop will be restricted by all your pawns. Trading your dark-squared bishop, though, would leave you with very little reinforcement on the dark squares. This is something else you need to bear in mind when thinking about which pieces to trade.

Black's pawn breaks in this position would likely be these:

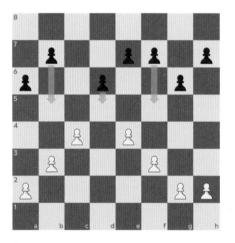

⬆ Again, this depends on what reinforcements both Black and White have on the squares in question. Black will need to find these pawn breaks—something we call **counterplay**, which is when the opponent responds to your forward progress with threats/an attack of their own—otherwise White has a really strong structure here that will be difficult for Black to break through.

That position is a little more open. Let's look at another one:

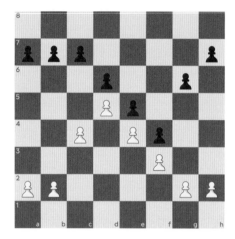

⬆ This is from the King's Indian Defense, one of the most complex systems in chess. Oftentimes space is also a factor when thinking about pawn structures. We talked about space earlier, and how it's ideal to take up more space than your opponent. In this position, Black has more space on the kingside and White has more space on the queenside, which is why White will try to rely on . . .

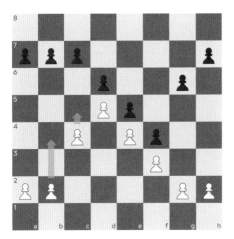

↑ ... these pawn breaks, which undermine Black's pawn structure and create space for White's other pieces. (Note that White is advancing pawns away from where White's king has usually castled, behind the g and h pawns—you don't want to push pawns protecting your king as it will leave your king vulnerable.) Meanwhile, Black will focus on ...

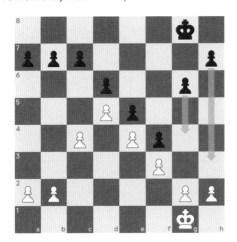

↑ ... pushing pawns on the other side to attack White's king.

Here's another example:

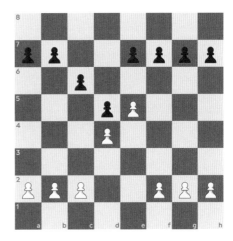

↑ This is from the Caro-Kann, Advance Variation. White has more central space, which is going to be good for restricting the movement of Black's pieces, while Black has pawn breaks ...

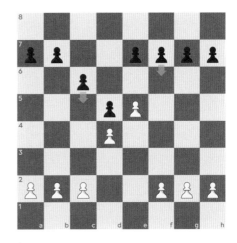

↑ ... with c5 and f6, trying to chip away at White's central structure. These are the obvious pawn breaks in this position because they are the only way for Black to attack White's pawns and undermine the structure.

These are just a few examples—there are many more—that show it's important to think about how your pawns are positioned in the opening, learn the ideal pawn structures associated with the openings you play, and understand the balance of pawns on the light and dark squares, particularly how pawns interact with the other pieces you have on the board. Pawns are the fence defending your position but are also crucial to defending your pieces farther up the board and creating attacking opportunities with pawn breaks.

It's important to not just talk about pawn structures in the opening, though. In any position in chess, it's crucial to recognize which pawns are together, sometimes called **pawn clusters** or **pawn islands**. Look at this position:

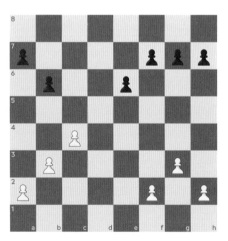

♟ Here both sides have two pawn clusters or islands. Black has a cluster of four on the kingside versus White's cluster of three—we would call this a **kingside majority**. Conversely,

White has a group of three queenside pawns versus Black's cluster of two, so it has a **queenside majority**. Why is this important? Well, understanding where you have a pawn majority will help you form plans in the end-game—a pawn majority, if advanced correctly and supported by your other pieces, will give you a better chance of getting a pawn to the other side of the board and promoting it to a queen.

Another common concept related to mid-dlegame or endgame pawn structures is an **isolated pawn**, which is where a pawn stands alone with no pawns on the neighboring files:

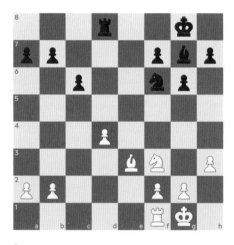

♟ In this case, White's d pawn doesn't have a neighbor to the left or right and thus is isolated. Isolated pawns can be either good or bad. They are better if you have a bunch of other pieces that can help defend the pawn, but also use the space around them to attack. The position here is the reverse. White has traded off quite a few pieces. The isolated pawn is currently protected by White's bishop and knight but really has no forward mobility—Black's rook pressures the pawn and Black's rook, knight, and c pawn completely cover the d5 square, so a lot would have to change for White's isolated pawn to be able to move even a single square.

This is known as a **blockade**, which is when a pawn cannot move forward because the opponent either occupies or controls the square in front. In this position, Black will try to trade off or move White's pieces that are defending the isolated pawn, at which point they will capture it and be up a pawn. Therefore, an isolated pawn can be an asset or a liability; it depends how you handle it and whether it poses more of a problem for your opponent than it does for you (i.e., if your pieces are stuck defending the pawn, this restricts your game play).

You also need to know about something called a **backwards pawn**:

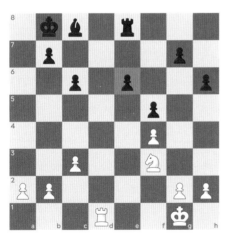

✎ In this position, the e6 pawn for Black is a backwards pawn. A backwards pawn is not quite isolated—it can have neighbors—but it has no forward mobility and is not defended by another pawn. In this case, White completely controls the e5 square with their f4 pawn and knight on f3 so Black cannot push the pawn forward. If Black's e6 pawn goes forward, it won't be traded but rather will be captured for free. Black has insufficient support of the pawn to push it forward and make it an even trade when White captures it. So, it's stuck backwards and is weak, meaning it constantly needs defending by other pieces, which in turn restricts the freedom of those other pieces.

Another pawn-related concept is **doubled pawns**:

⬆ This is a position from the Petrov Defense, Classical Variation. This position has been reached hundreds of thousands of times. You'll notice White has two pawns on the c file—they are doubled. This happened because the knights were traded on the c3 square and White recaptured Black's knight with their d pawn. Doubled pawns are a controversial topic.

Some people might say doubled pawns are weak—they are less mobile and because pawns capture diagonally, the pawn behind is not protecting the pawn in front—but it's not always the case that doubled pawns are weak. Doubled pawns can add both extra defense to a particular area of the board and potentially boost your spatial control and piece mobility. Doubling your pawns can also open up lines for your other pieces. In the previous position, White's doubled pawns mean White's bishops see lots of squares and so too does White's queen.

Here is an example of some bad doubled pawns:

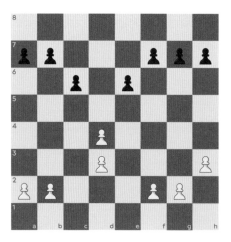

🖊 Not only are White's central pawns doubled, they are also isolated. Neither of them is defended by other pawns, neither can move, and they will be very hard for White to protect from being captured. These pawns are a weakness in the position and are technically doubled, backwards, and isolated! So, a really bad position for White. (Don't even get me started on tripled pawns, which can happen and should be avoided at all costs . . .)

Finally, it's important to talk about **pawn chains**, which means a line of pawns, each defended by another pawn behind it, excluding the pawn at the very bottom of the chain:

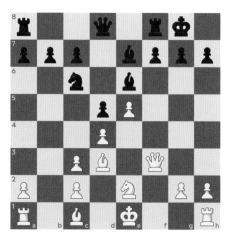

⬆ This is a position from the Vienna Opening. You will notice that White has a pawn chain stretching from c3 to d4 to e5. This is a very strong pawn chain; each pawn is defended by the one behind it, and the c3 pawn is defended by White's knight on e2. This pawn chain gains space for White and restricts Black's movement.

Here is another example of a pawn chain:

⬆ This is from the French Defense. Both White and Black have strong pawn chains here. Because Black's pawn chain leads toward the queenside, Black will focus their attack on that side of White's position—the pawn chain is a stronghold and space advantage for Black. On the other hand, White's pawn chain gives them lots of space and attacking opportunities on the kingside. This could allow something called a **pawn storm**, which is when you march clusters of pawns toward a castled enemy king (you should really only launch pawns forward when those pawns aren't defending your own king, though, which is why pawn storms are most common in games where players have castled on opposite sides).

This is the handful of different pawn concepts that you need to be thinking about in any position. Pawns are the lowest-value piece on the board, and so sometimes players don't value them highly enough. One pawn is worth a single point but together all your pawns are worth eight points—only a queen is worth more!

Bishops and Knights

Bishop versus knight is a fascinating debate. They are both worth three points but there is an argument to be made that a bishop is worth fractionally more. Both Bobby Fischer and Garry Kasparov—two of the greatest chess players of all time—gave the bishop a value somewhere between 3.15 and 3.25 points, versus 3.0 points for the knight. Let's try to understand why:

⬆ A bishop in a central square of an empty board sees thirteen squares. A knight, on the other hand . . .

♟ . . . has eight moves.

Furthermore, there are situations where a bishop could completely trap a knight:

♟ In this position, all of the moves available to the Black knight are highlighted. The bishop covers all of them, meaning it fully traps the Black knight. The reverse isn't true: there are no situations on an empty board where a knight could trap a bishop.

A bishop can move from one corner of the board to the other in one move. A knight would take four or five moves to do the same. Bishops can be like lightning bolts, making them extremely useful for long-range attacks or bolstering a queen's attack from a distance, particularly in open positions or endgames where fewer pieces block a bishop's vision.

One drawback of a bishop is that they only see half the board. Your light-squared bishop only sees the light squares and vice versa for your dark-squared bishop. Both knights, on the other hand, can (in theory) visit all sixty-four squares on the board. A knight is not as good as a bishop in terms of long-range capabilities, but knights have other qualities. A knight is the only piece that can hop over other pieces, both yours and your opponent's. Knight forks are also particularly dangerous if they are forking pieces (that hopefully aren't opposing knights), because the L shape of a knight's attack is different from how the other pieces attack.

As we've talked about before, bishops prefer an open board. Take this position:

⬆ White's light-squared bishop will never see the light of day. It's going to take a long time and lots of moves before it can get out or see any of the board. White's dark-squared bishop can move one square to d2—otherwise Black's pawns cover every other square the dark-squared bishop might move to (e3, f4, and g5).

The more pawns on the board and the more a position is closed, the less effective bishops become. Knights are generally okay in any kind of position—they're more like jacks-of-all-trades. They can hop over pieces

and pawn blockades and can reroute easier than bishops in closed positions. For example, in the previous position either of White's knights could get to the c4 square in two or three moves; I have no idea how White could get their light-squared bishop there in fewer than ten moves, if not more.

Compare that to this position from the Danish Gambit:

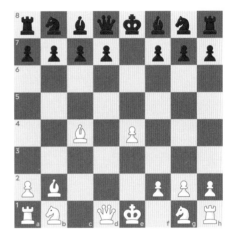

⬆ Here White's bishops are salivating like happy dogs staring at your steak dinner. They see lots of squares and stare at the pawns surrounding Black's king, ready to deal some serious damage. Having said that, Black's dark-squared bishop has lots of space to move into and could quickly give a check on b4.

The point is that bishops love being able to move and love open positions. Knights don't mind either way. Another distinction between the two is that bishops can be far away from the main action and still be useful:

⬆ You'll notice in this position that Black's light-squared bishop is extremely useful. It stands all the way over on b7 but controls the entire diagonal down to h1, preventing White's king from crossing onto those light squares.

The White knight, however, needs to be much closer to the action to be useful. Knights are strongest on **outposts**. An outpost is a square—typically in your opponent's territory—where you can position a piece in a protected spot where it cannot be removed (i.e., by an enemy pawn or attacking it) or traded off. Nothing of equal or lesser value can get rid of it. In the above position, the White knight is on an outpost. Black has no pawns that can attack the knight and Black's light-squared bishop can do nothing because the knight is on a dark square. This makes the knight very powerful, planted in the enemy position. A bishop can also be on an outpost, but outposts tend to maximize the value of

a knight more than a bishop. That's because a knight can still hop backward over the pawn defending it, whereas a pawn defending a bishop actually blocks the bishop from seeing along that particular diagonal. Bishops like lots of open space.

Let's not forget that knights can also work together, combining to attack or control the same square. This is never true of a bishop pair since they operate on different color complexes. Look at this position:

⬆ This comes from the English Opening. Both of White's knights are covering the d5 square in the center. This reinforces White's control of the square—White could put one of the knights there, defended by the other. Bishops can't ever do this.

The fact that knights can work together like this is definitely a plus for the knight pair.

However, having both bishops in a situation where your opponent has lost one or both of their bishops is generally considered good, particularly at the highest level. For example, if you are the only player in the game with a light-squared bishop, then you have more control over the light squares than your opponent. On the other hand, if you are down a bishop or two, the way to deal with this problem goes back to pawn structures:

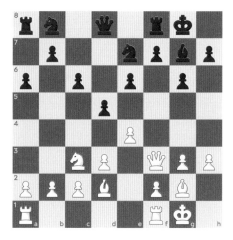

⬆ In this position, Black has traded off their light-squared bishop for White's knight. To counteract White's control of the light squares, Black has put all eight of their pawns on light squares (remember pawn complexes on page 209). This prevents White's light-squared bishop from moving very much, even if White's queen and e4 pawn move out of the way. White has the bishop pair, but the advantage of the bishop pair is not felt because

Black is rock solid on the light squares. If the game develops further and Black loses this light-squared blockade . . .

⬆ . . . you can see how White's light-squared bishop has become more active. This position is nice for White because White's bishops can cut across the board in way that Black's knights cannot.

Knights have to get close to a bishop to threaten it. Think about it like range in boxing: the person with longer range can do damage from farther away, while the person with less range has to get in closer and potentially put themselves at more risk. Bishop pairs and knight pairs both have their merits, but on balance bishops tend to be slightly more powerful, especially as the board begins to clear. This is why I always warn people against giving up a bishop for a knight; it can seem like an even trade, but don't trade your bishop for an enemy knight without good reason.

Rooks

From the starting position in chess, your rooks are in the corners. Rooks are generally considered more relevant to the middlegame and endgame than the opening. They're worth five points because they really do possess a lot of power:

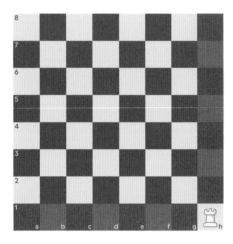

⬆ A rook in the center of an empty board can move to fourteen squares. A rook in the very corner of the board . . .

⬆ . . . also sees fourteen squares, which is part of why a rook is better than a bishop or knight. A bishop or knight sees far fewer squares from the very corner than they do from the center.

A rook will always be better than a knight or bishop in an endgame. You can checkmate with a king and rook, which you cannot do with a king and bishop or king and knight. Rooks tend to come into the game a little bit later than pawns, bishops, knights, and even the queen. Let's consider this position:

🡹 Here both sides have developed quite naturally—White's position somewhat resembles our golden moves from Chapter One. After the other pieces are developed, rooks want to find the central files in the opening. This tends to be the extent of a rook's part in the opening, supporting the other pieces along the center files, each rook protecting the other. In addition to getting your king to safety, castling naturally helps bring at least one of your rooks toward the center.

One of the toughest questions in chess is where to place each rook in the opening. Which rook should go to which file? More often than not you want your rooks in the middle, but that's not necessarily always the case. For example, if another file is particularly open (i.e., there are few or no pieces blocking the file), you always want a rook controlling that file. Likewise, if you see that, in the coming moves, a particular file will likely open up by trades or movement, it might make sense to place a rook on that file so that when the position clears the rook becomes very powerful.

Rooks love open files:

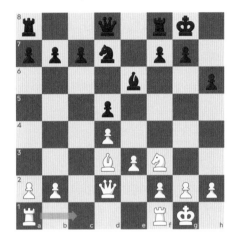

🡹 In this position, the c file is very open. Putting a rook there will mean that rook controls lots of squares and constantly pressures the enemy position. In this case the rook from a1 should slide over to c1 because if the f1 rook did, it would squish its friend in the corner!

Rooks are most powerful when they work together. We talked about doubled pawns—doubled rooks are also an important concept to be aware of. Take a look at this position:

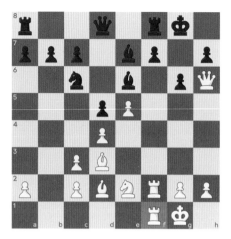

♟ Here the White rooks are **doubled** up on the f file, which is a dangerous battery. Doubling your rooks can be a powerful thing to do when the rooks have a clear line of sight to the enemy position.

Another way in which rooks can combine to incredible effect can be seen in this position:

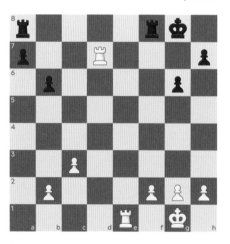

♟ Here White has the chance to double their rooks not vertically but horizontally . . .

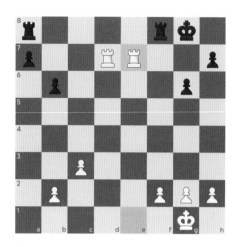

♟ . . . with the move rook to e7. Rooks on the seventh or second rank is a particularly strong tactic in the endgame. Here on the seventh rank, they become like a buzz saw, threatening both of Black's outside pawns while also threatening . . .

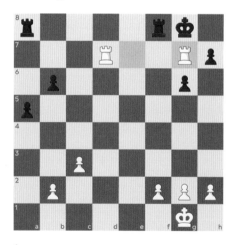

♟ . . . to checkmate the king with a series of checks resulting in . . .

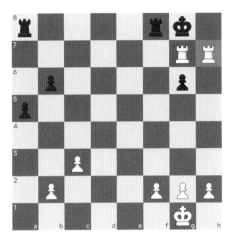

♟ . . . a final position that looks like this. Black can't do anything since White used their rooks to check the king repeatedly, first on g7, then on h7, then again on g7 (but this time with the other rook), resulting in the checkmate shown.

So, rook batteries—either up and down or horizontally—can be devastating and are generally incredibly effective.

Another thing to bear in mind regarding rooks is a concept called **relative value**. Throughout a game of chess, a rook isn't always what I would call a five-point rook, which is a rook at its most powerful. Oftentimes a rook can be sacrificed for a lesser piece if it means getting some kind of compensation, either short-term or long-term—short-term might mean winning extra material or opening your opponent's king to a devastating attack, while long-term might mean damaging their pawn structure. Take this example:

♙ Black is up two pawns in this position. Black should have the advantage but White plays the move . . .

♟ . . . rook takes f6, because—even though a rook is worth five and a knight only three—the resulting position when Black recaptures . . .

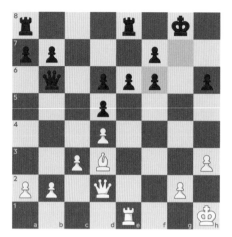

♟ ... opens up Black's king and exposes it to a potentially fatal attack ...

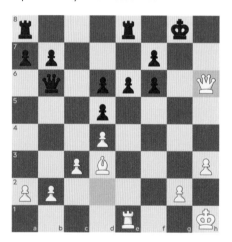

♟ ... after White gets in there with the queen. It's not over yet, though. Let's say Black ...

♟ ... blocks the White bishop with the move f5. In this case, White should use another attacking technique with a rook, called a **rook lift**. This is a common and powerful idea with a rook, which involves moving a rook up and across so that it joins a potential attack.

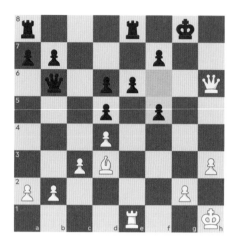

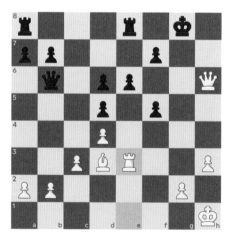

♟ Here the rook lift begins with rook up to e3. White's plan from here will be to get the rook to g3, which will be checkmate.

Rooks generally come into the game around move ten, sometimes earlier and sometimes later, but mostly they are pieces reserved for the latter parts of the game. Here is a bonus example where we combine some of these rook-related concepts:

♟ This is a variation of the London System. Here White has waited for Black to castle their king and now launches their flank pawn on the h file.

✦ The flank pawn marches forward, supported by the rook and the queen. This is another way to activate your rook that doesn't involve sliding it to the middle; throwing a flank pawn forward into the attack can open up the file for your rook to become more powerful. You'll notice that Black has a pawn and knight attacking White's flank pawn in the previous position . . .

♟ . . . but the plan is actually to sacrifice the rook to end up in this position. White has a crushing advantage here despite having sacrificed the rook for the knight, with the queen hovering ominously by the Black king's position, White's light-squared bishop ready to move to d3, and White's other rook potentially lining up behind the queen when White castles long and moves their bishop and knight off the back rank.

The Queen

We've looked at the Scholar's Mate and touched on how bringing your queen out early isn't the best idea. For the long-term development of your game, it's not ideal to bring your queen out before developing your other pieces. You have to understand that, at the start of the game, you are going up against 39 points of material. That army of pieces can easily deal with one hostile queen. A queen can lead an attack, but it needs a supporting cast. It's like a star player on a sports team; it might put up incredible numbers, but without a great supporting team, it's not going to win any championships.

Having said all that, it's worth knowing that there are ways you can trick your opponent with your queen early on, particularly at the beginner level (but less so as you move into intermediate territory). As your Elo increases, your opponents will no longer fall for any tricks associated with bringing out the queen early and they will likely punish you for it.

It's much more worthwhile to deepen your understanding of how the queen can work with other pieces and to improve your ability to recognize certain tactical patterns involving the queen, which will be very useful as you progress in intermediate play. First off, a queen and a rook—queens love batteries with rooks:

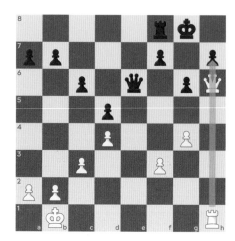

⬆ Here the queen and rook are lined up together and are about to deliver checkmate. Queens and rooks can also combine from different angles. The rook could be lined up vertically and the queen diagonally, for example.

Something that makes the queen so strong is that it combines the powers of the rook and bishop. In many ways the queen, with the right support, can do damage up close *and* from a distance, which is what makes the queen so dangerous and so annoying to an opponent. If a queen finds a way into your position, as the White queen has in the Black position above, it's going to be disastrous for the person defending.

On the next board, the queen forms a battery with the bishop, as we've seen before:

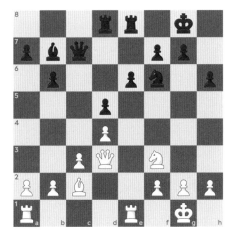

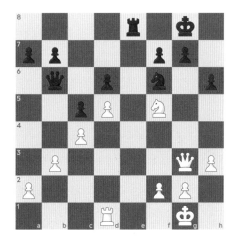

⬆ You might be bored of seeing this but, as my communications professor used to say back in my freshman year of college, "I know I'm repeating myself: repetition for emphasis." White has a queen and bishop battery aimed at the h7 square beside Black's king. At the moment, the Black knight defends that square, but this is why the queen is so powerful: it is a constant menace even from far away, and it also patrols other squares at the same time and can move to the other side of the board in a flash.

Queen and knight, if coordinated correctly, is the most dangerous combination in chess because it combines the power of literally every piece. The knight is the only piece that moves uniquely and can do things the queen can't. Take this position:

⬆ Between White's queen and knight in this position, White is threatening to take three different Black pawns. The knight and the queen both target d6 and g7 (which is checkmate, incidentally, so obviously the best move) but also the knight is threatening to take h6. Despite this pawn appearing to be defended, Black's g7 pawn is pinned to the king by White's queen on the same file and so wouldn't be able to recapture the White knight if it took the h6 pawn.

This just goes to show how brutal a combination the queen and knight make. They work together extremely well and can attack multiple things together at the same time. Of course, unlike with a bishop or a rook, there is no straightaway or battery possible with a queen and knight. With these two pieces, you'll always be attacking from different angles. And, as we learned in the previous section, a knight tends to need to be up close to be an effective attacker or supporter.

⬆ Of course, a queen on its own is still exceptionally powerful, capable of attacking multiple things at the same time. Forks are particularly common with a queen, and one of the most effective is the fork that is both check and an attack on a loose piece. In this position, if the queen slides to a4 then it's check; Black will have to block or escape the check, and the queen will capture the bishop on the next move (this goes back to the CCA checklist—always look for checks!).

It can happen in later parts of the game, too, as in this position:

⬆ Here Black is threatening checkmate on g2 (queen takes g2 is mate, the queen protected by the knight on h4), but it's White's turn to move. If you follow the CCA checklist—checks, captures, attacks—White has a move that wins material and stops the threat. That move is . . .

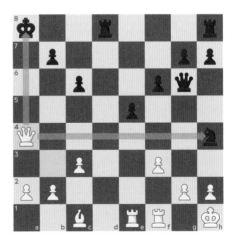

⬆ . . . queen to a4. This attacks the king four squares away and the knight seven squares away in the opposite direction. This just shows the awesome power of the queen. Black will have to get out of check, after which White can gobble up the knight.

The vision of the queen is incredible. In the previous position, a rook would also be able to deliver the same fork, but a rook wouldn't have been able to make the diagonal move from b3 to a4. This shows what an incredible combination of multiple pieces the queen really is.

Needless to say, you should try to be using your queen in an aggressive, attacking capacity rather than as a defensive piece. You don't want your queen stuck defending your king and unable to move, since then you've deprived yourself of your most powerful attacker. At the same time, given that the queen is so powerful, you need to be careful with how early you bring it out and where you place it. Getting your queen trapped or blundering it will often lead to you losing the game if your opponent still has their queen. There will be certain situations where there's an opportunity to trade your queen for your opponent's. We're going to talk about trades next, but for now, the decision on whether or not to trade queens depends on the specific situation in the game. Will trading the queens be beneficial to your position? Are you up material or down material? If the latter, trading off your most powerful piece will only make it more likely you lose.

Your queen is your most potent and hostile piece but needs to be handled carefully. You'll become better equipped at handling your queen the right way as you play more chess and improve your game. You will blunder your queen many times as you climb the ratings ladder. It's painful but all part of learning how to play most effectively with your queen. Since your queen is your second most valuable piece after your king, you need to learn to always be checking that your queen is out of danger just as much as you do with your king.

Trading Pieces

Now that we've studied pieces individually, it's time to discuss when, why, and how to trade them (or not!). Exchanging pieces in chess—specifically, when to trade and when not to trade—is one of the trickiest skills to master. When they first start playing chess, players tend to only evaluate whether a trade is good or bad depending on the value of the material. A pawn for a pawn, a bishop for a knight, a rook for a rook—these are all technically even trades. But there is much more that goes into the value of a piece in any given situation on the chessboard than the numerical value. To get better at chess, you *must* be able to properly evaluate whether or not to make a trade.

Before we get into specifics, it's important to know about trades in openings. Just as you have to learn the development, variations, and pawn structures of openings, you have to understand the trades that occur in the openings you play—and whether or not you should be making certain trades in your openings. Let's look at a basic example:

♟ This is the Scotch Opening. Here Black will . . .

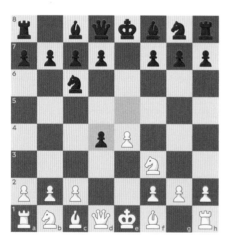

♙ . . . capture the d pawn with their e pawn. If Black doesn't do this, White will completely dominate the center. In capturing the pawn, Black forces White to respond, which might be to capture the Black pawn with the knight, which in turn might lead to a trade of knights.

The point here is that trades are slightly different in the early stages of the game. Some of them have to happen and are usually the best move in order for the opening to proceed in optimal fashion. Again, this all comes down to learning and studying your openings in detail. The position above is interesting as it continues to develop:

♙ Now White has captured the Black pawn with their knight. Black has the option to trade the knights but that's considered a bad move from Black's perspective.

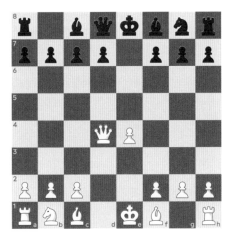

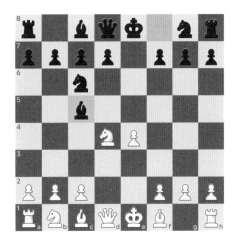

♙ This is because Black will end up with no pieces developed, while White will have a queen in the center and easy development of their other pieces. This exchange has given White too much. The pawn exchange was necessary to stop White from controlling the center, but this exchange traded off Black's only active piece. Sure, White's queen is out early, but here she is completely safe. Remember, the point of the opening is to develop your pieces—developing them only to immediately trade them off means you are losing developed pieces.

♙ Rather than trade the knights, it's better for Black to do something in this position called **keeping the tension**, which means allowing pieces to see one another without rushing in to capture. This is a skill you'll develop more as you get better at the game. Here Black has developed their bishop and is now forcing White to either protect or move their knight. White's best move is *also* to not capture Black's knight, but rather, to continue developing with bishop to e3.

A lot of beginners simply trade everything whenever they can without thinking strategically about it or evaluating whether it improves their position. The opening stage is slightly different in terms of trades because some are necessary and part of the theory of those openings.

Another example can be found in the Semi-Slav Defense of the Queen's Gambit:

⬆ You'll notice here that White's c4 pawn and Black's d5 pawn see each other and either could capture the other. But neither side wants to do that. If White captures, Black's position will unlock further and allow Black quick development by recapturing with the e pawn, clearing space for the light-squared bishop to develop a couple of moves later. If Black captures on c4, White will recapture with their light-squared bishop, developing the bishop to a very active square and obtaining a central pawn majority.

Instead, the players keep the tension and develop around that tension. Opening trades are different than middlegame trades and it's important to learn the trades that can, should, and shouldn't happen in your openings.

Let's move on to trades beyond the opening. When thinking about whether or not to trade, consider the positives, negatives, or equalities of that trade—both for yourself and your opponent. In thinking about the positives, would the trade benefit just one side? Would the trade benefit both sides? Would both sides be happy with the trade? Will one side be happier than the other? And on the flip side of the positives are the negatives—is a trade bad for one player, or bad for both in different ways? And some trades are just balanced.

An important thing to understand is that every trade changes the position. This can mean certain pieces seeing things they didn't see before or pieces controlling or having access to squares they didn't have before. It is therefore crucial not just to evaluate the material value of one piece being traded for another, but also to evaluate the big picture of how the trade changes the board—and which side most benefits from the change in position.

On the next page is a simple table about when you should and shouldn't trade. This isn't meant to be followed in absolutely every case—there will always be exceptions—but it works as a general starting point.

Do Trade . . .	Don't Trade . . .
. . . if you are up material in order to simplify the position down into a winning endgame.	. . . when you are down material. The fewer pieces you have, the less chance you have of finding a way back into the game.
. . . to gain certain positional advantages, such as forcing your opponent to double their pawns, creating a weakness, opening up the enemy king, trading a bad piece for a good piece (meaning trading off a very active opposing piece for a less active piece of your own).	. . . a very good piece (an active or dangerous piece of your own) for a bad piece (an opposing piece that isn't taking part in the game) even if it wins you some small material, like a pawn.
. . . when you are under attack and trading off the attacking pieces saves you.	. . . when you are attacking and trading off the attacking pieces would mean the end of the attack.

A good rule of thumb: do not trade unless you can verbally explain what benefit it would give to your position. If you're trading just because you can, it's not good enough. You need to be able to explain yourself. Don't become addicted to trading—equal in material doesn't mean equal positionally. At the same time, you can't live or die by steadfast rules in chess. Some people say things like "I never trade queens" or "I always trade bishops for knights because knights are super tricky and I can never predict how they're going to move." Chess can't be played with generalizations like these. The chessboard doesn't care about you or your opinions of the game; each position determines whether a trade is good or bad for both sides.

Let's take a look at a few concrete examples, starting with this:

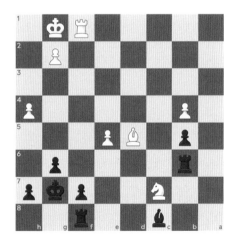

⬆ This is from one of my own blitz games. I have the Black pieces and I'm up two points of material—I have a rook for a knight, which is called an exchange up. And so here I played the move . . .

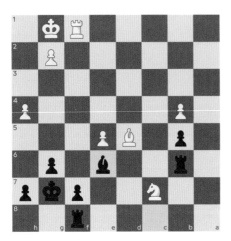

🨋 . . . bishop to e6. I want to trade bishops because I'm up material. My opponent's bishop is more active than mine and, furthermore, when my f7 pawn recaptures the white bishop, my rook will open up on the f file. We might then trade rooks and simplify down to an endgame where my material advantage is preserved and I can win. My opponent didn't want to trade the bishops, but we ended up . . .

🨋 . . . in this position, where my opponent is stuck. If my opponent moves their rook, my b6 rook will take the White bishop. Here I attacked . . .

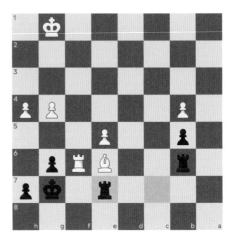

🨋 . . . the bishop with my other rook, forcing the bishop to move. That would allow a trade of rooks and I'd be up a rook versus bishop in the endgame, which is winning. Rather than playing that situation out, my opponent just resigned the game.

That's an example of pushing hard for an exchange. I was up material and knew that if the position simplified it would lead to a winning endgame.

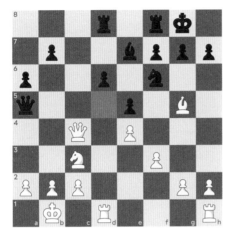

⬆ Here's another example where we can make a trade that gives a positional advantage. We learned about outposts earlier in this chapter. In this position, the d5 square would be a great outpost for White's knight, but currently it would simply be traded by Black's knight on f6. So, White should . . .

⬆ . . . capture Black's knight with the bishop. More often than not, bishop for knight is not a great trade—we explored earlier why bishops are considered slightly better than knights. Here, however, after Black recaptures White's bishop with their bishop . . .

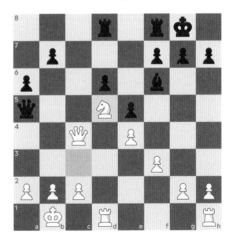

⬆ . . . White can plant their knight on that powerful d5 outpost. Black's remaining bishop will never be able to remove it; in fact, Black's only pieces that could remove the knight are the rook and the queen, which would mean giving up pieces of greater value to capture the knight.

That is an example of a beneficial positional exchange. Let's look at another example where we can create a weakness in the opponent's position:

⬆ Here Black has offered White a queen trade. White could capture and Black would recapture with the b7 pawn and it would be nine points for nine. That doesn't make it an even trade, though. We need to understand how the board changes. There are players who say they never trade queens, but you shouldn't have rules like that. The best move here for White is to trade queens because, after Black recaptures with the pawn . . .

⬆ . . . White slides the rook over and targets Black's c6 pawn. We learned about rooks loving open files and we learned about backwards pawns. Black is going to find it difficult to defend that pawn in the long term.

This is how trading to create a weakness can be very effective. In the above position, even if Black pushes the pawn to allow it to be defended by the Black bishop on e7, both of Black's center pawns will be vulnerable to pressure and tactics, and Black will find it hard to keep them both.

Now let's look at trading when you're under attack:

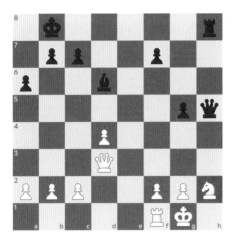

🔼 Here Black is ready to checkmate White with queen takes h2. If White moves their knight, it's checkmate on h1. White's only move here . . .

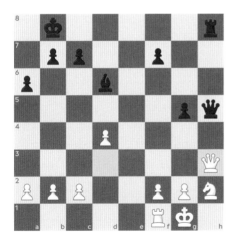

🔼 . . . is queen to h3. When the queens are traded, Black's rook will also pick up White's g2 pawn (which will have moved to h3 to capture Black's queen), but losing a pawn is better than being checkmated. You'll see how

once the queens are traded and the Black rook has captured the White pawn . . .

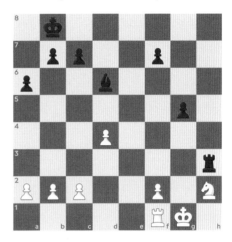

🔼 . . . Black's attack has really fizzled out. There is no checkmate threat anymore and White can get the rook and knight out and try to fight back. This is particularly true when there's an opportunity to trade off your opponent's queen when the queen is leading the attack; once the queen is traded, often the attack will be over.

Those are some examples of good trades, whether for positional advantage, creating weaknesses, or stopping a devastating attack. Now let's look at some examples of when *not* to trade. The first scenario when you shouldn't trade doesn't even need an example: don't trade when you're down material. Unless there is some immediate, huge reason for making even trades when down material, it should just be common sense not to do this. If you think about it, if you are down two or three points of material and then trade all the way down, you'll be left with just a king and your opponent will have two or three points of material—which means you'll lose. Imagine you're down a player in a soccer match; you wouldn't accept an offer to take away another of your players for one of your opponent's, because the opponent will still always have more.

Another time you shouldn't be trading is when you're giving up a good piece for a bad piece. The funniest example of this can happen in the third move of the London System:

⬆ Technically White's bishop on f4 is worth three points. Black's knight on b8 is also—technically—worth three points. But bishop takes b8 . . .

⬆ . . . is a horrible, ridiculous move. You're giving up a powerful, developed bishop for a knight that is asleep and sitting on its home square. A beginner might argue this is three for three but it's not; you've traded a great piece for a bad one. Don't ever do this.

A more sophisticated example of this can be seen here:

Here the White knight is dominant on d6. It's a beast. It *could* capture the bishop sitting on c8 but there is absolutely no good reason to do so. You could say bishops are better than knights—but not this knight! This knight is wedged in your opponent's position and causing problems. Black's bishop, on the other hand, is not good—it's on its home square and isn't threatening or defending anything important. It isn't participating in the game at all and White should be happy to leave it there. This would be a terrible trade for White.

Don't just trade because you can. Don't just trade because you've heard bishops are better than knights, either. Not all knights are equal. The position dictates everything. This is why there is so much more that goes into evaluating piece value than the number of points. In the previous position, Black would love to trade for the knight on d6 because it's such a thorn in their position.

There's one other thing we should look at before moving on. There are certain situations—such as the following—where a player has the option to trade off a bishop and knight (six points total) for a rook and pawn (also six points):

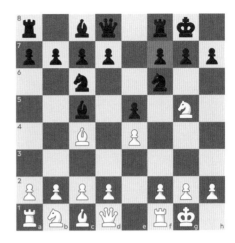

Here White's bishop and knight both see Black's pawn on f7. White can play . . .

. . . knight takes f7.

⬆ Black then retakes with the rook, White captures the rook with the bishop, and Black . . . recaptures with the king, leaving this position. Technically, this is six points for six. But it's not—six is not equal to six *in this case.* Knight and bishop are two unique, powerful tools. Rooks and pawns aren't, especially in the early stages of the game. Trading a bishop and knight for a rook and pawn is not a good trade—you're just down a piece, even if material is technically equal. And look at what this trade has done to White's position. White has no pieces developed and Black has three.

If you cannot explain the benefit of a trade—whether creating a weakness, simplifying a position down, or opening up your opponent's king—I would always recommend keeping the tension. Don't rush into trades if they don't improve your position or, worse still, only benefit your opponent.

Checklist

To finish, we're going to bring together as many of these concepts as possible to help you understand how to find good moves and make plans in chess. For this I'm going to use some more examples from my own games. You'll recall the CCA checklist—checks, captures, attacks—from the intermediate tactics chapter, but now we're going to add some more layers.

Imagine our opponent makes a move. Immediately we need to ask ourselves, "What does my opponent want?" That's not always going to be easy to answer, though there might be an immediate threat or idea that makes it more obvious. Correctly evaluating this will help you make correct decisions. If you don't successfully evaluate what your opponent wants—or don't even try—you may miss threats on your pieces or position and instead react incorrectly. This is something you need to practice as you play more chess. Sometimes it's easier to only focus on what you're doing but you will never improve beyond a certain level if you play like this.

In every position, we are looking for checks, captures, and attacks. Scan for them before you make any move. Are they there? Then evaluate them. Do the checks lead anywhere or are they just checks for no reason? Are the captures good or bad for your position? Are the attacks easily escaped or, worse, might they help your opponent? Always be looking for weaknesses in your opponent's position. Are there loosely guarded pieces in your opponent's position to which you could add more pressure? If you have none of these options, which can happen, then you look for moves which improve your position. What does this mean? It could be moving a piece to a more active square or taking more space with a forward pawn move.

So, that's the checklist. Let's try to apply it in some example positions, starting with one of my own games:

⬆ My opponent, playing Black, has just pushed their pawn to e5. So, what does my opponent want? My opponent wants to push their e pawn again and fork my queen and bishop. Running through the checklist, I see that I don't have any checks. In terms of captures, I could capture the e pawn with my d pawn. However, if I do that my opponent will retake with their knight and *still* fork my queen and bishop. Rather than trading and activating my opponent's knight, I simply avoided the danger . . .

⬆ . . . by sliding my queen back. I maintain a strong position and I don't open up the center of the board for my opponent's pieces. I keep the tension with my center pawns and I don't let my opponent's knight or bishop on b7 get more active. Also, had I gone forward with my queen (to f5, let's say), my opponent could have taken my weak e3 pawn! I am accepting that I am not the one calling the shots in this position; rather, I am fending off danger and staying afloat. I went on to win from here—not solely because of queen to f2, obviously.

Here's another example from one of my games:

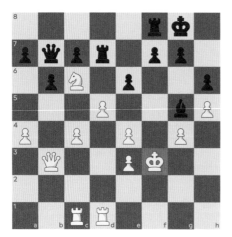

🔼 You'll notice my king is on f3—he seems to have partied too hard and stumbled into the middle of the board. Suddenly my opponent attacks with . . .

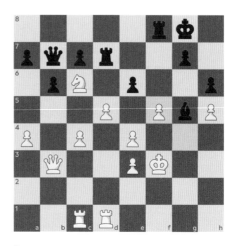

🔼 I capture that pawn with my g pawn. My opponent captures with their e pawn and instead of capturing with my e pawn, I . . .

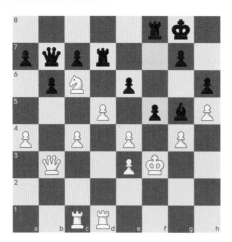

🔼 . . . the move pawn to f5. What does my opponent want? To open up their rook on the f file, attacking my king. So, what do I do?

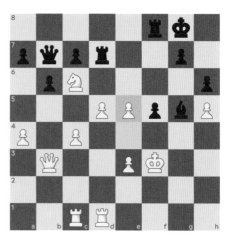

🔼 . . . push my e pawn forward. I make sure the f file stays closed, not allowing the rook a clear line of sight down to my king. I also now have a passed pawn—a pawn that cannot be stopped by any enemy pawns.

Even though I made the right decision here, I went on to lose this game because chess is brutal. I managed to mess it up a little bit later.

Here's another example involving trading and decision making:

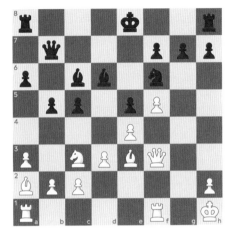

⬆ In this position, it isn't obvious what my opponent, playing Black, wants. It's difficult to identify what Black wants because White has a very strong position. Checks, captures, and attacks come back fruitless. So I have a better position, but who cares? The game doesn't just end here—what do I do next? Seeing there was no immediate danger to my position, I went to trade . . .

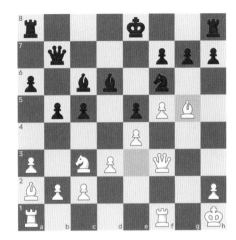

⬆ . . . my bishop for their knight by moving my bishop to g5, preparing to capture the Black knight on my next move. I did this because it meant damaging my opponent's structure . . .

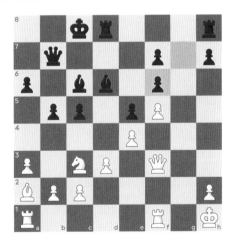

⬆ . . . after they recaptured my bishop with the pawn on f6, while also removing Black's control of the d5 square. Then I decided to force another trade with the move . . .

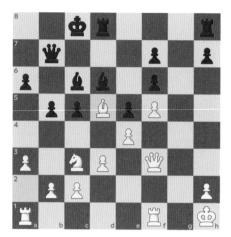

♟ . . . bishop to d5. I want my knight on the d5 square—which will be an outpost and make the knight very problematic for Black. A couple of moves later and the position . . .

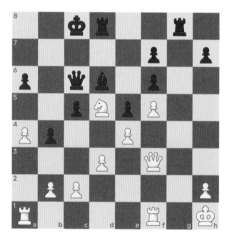

♟ . . . looked like this. My knight is completely dominant, and I won this game shortly afterward.

When there is no immediate pressure or threat from your opponent, look for ways to improve your position and impose your own game plan.

Now let's look at some positions I completely misevaluated:

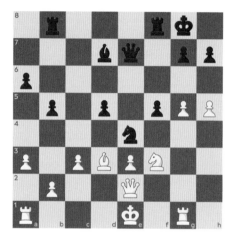

♟ Just using the checklist isn't enough—you have to apply it correctly. I had this position against a fellow International Master and thought the best thing to do was castle queenside, getting my king to safety. The problem was, I didn't think about what my opponent wanted. All of a sudden came the move . . .

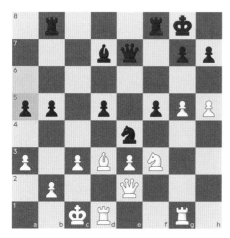

↑ ... a5, and on the next move came ...

↑ ... b4. I completely overlooked how significant the danger from those pawns was after castling on the queenside. Castling lost me the game—usually castling is about getting your king to safety, but in this case I castled right into Black's pawn storm.

The game ended a few moves later after Black ripped open my king's position and brought their other pieces to the party. I didn't anticipate what my opponent wanted—or what they might do once I had castled long.

Another funny example of my misevaluating was this position:

↑ I have the White pieces here and the position is totally equal. My rook on a4 is under attack from the Black pawn but—rather than retreat—I decide ...

... to move my rook to b4 and attack the Black pawn. What I failed to realize here is that my rook is now trapped ...

... bishop to f8 and traps my rook on b4. My rook has nowhere safe to run where it won't be captured by one of Black's pieces.

I went on to lose the game shortly thereafter—being lazy comes back to bite you very quickly. I needed to use the CCA checklist—from my opponent's perspective— to evaluate whether or not my plan was good. Instead, I casually attacked Black's pawn without thinking and suddenly I was losing.

The funniest example I have of my misevaluating was from a blitz game in which I was in a time scramble—I had maybe five or six seconds left on the clock here:

... after Black defends the pawn with rook to b8. I didn't look at checks, captures, attacks for my opponent. Next I move my other rook to a1, after which my opponent plays ...

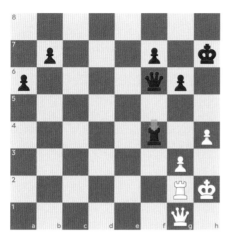

♟ I had the White pieces here against talented American prodigy Christopher Yoo. In this position, my opponent had played rook f4. Excited and thinking my opponent had blundered because of low time, I . . .

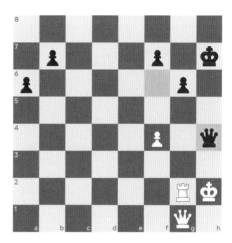

♟ . . . with the move queen takes h4. My opponent laid a trap for me and I fell for it. In hindsight, rook to f4 had another threat, which was to capture my h4 pawn anyway and result in the same checkmate.

In any case, I got checkmated because I did not look for checks for my opponent. I skipped the checklist—admittedly under huge time pressure—and lost in brutal fashion.

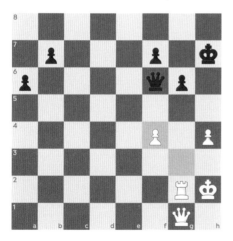

♟ . . . grabbed the rook with my pawn. I then got humiliatingly checkmated . . .

Summary

Pawns are the foundation of any chess position, resembling a fence between the two sides of pieces. Pawn structure is often determined by which opening both sides chose, and the ensuing position is characterized by various pawn breaks to fight for space, key squares for piece development, and overall control of the board.

We covered pawn structures, breaks, clusters, islands, majorities, complexes, blockades, chains, and storms in the first section of this chapter. Isn't it incredible that the humble pawn, worth a mere one point, is capable of being so incredibly important in the royal game?

The dichotomy between knights and bishops was on full display in this chapter, and similarly to the endgames we studied in Chapter Thirteen, a bishop prevails as a slight favorite over the knight. Bishops love an open position, particularly when one of the players possesses the "bishop pair." However, because a single bishop only has the ability to see thirty-two squares on a chessboard, a knight is a bit more flexible and can certainly put up a great fight against one bishop on the opposing set of squares. Bishops and knights both excel on outposts, though.

When faced with the option of trading a bishop for a knight, I would argue that it is not a good decision seven times out of ten. If you gain a tangible benefit—such as damaging a pawn structure or some tactical knockout—then by all means go for the exchange, but more often than not, the bishop will be superior in the long run.

Rooks are tricky! They start in the corners and frequently do not partake in the game at all until the late middle-game. I have played games where one of my rooks did not budge until my thirty-fifth turn—talk about a lazy employee! To successfully utilize rooks, you must connect them by completing development. At times you can utilize a rook lift to simply activate one of them on their own. However, if you want your rooks to work together, you should double them vertically down a file or horizontally on the opponent's 7th rank, where they will wreak havoc on a position.

Queens are like the dragons in *Game of Thrones*. It is no surprise they are the most powerful and valuable pieces on the board—they can seemingly do it all. Remember, on an empty board, a queen is able to see a maximum of twenty-seven squares—nearly half! Understanding the damage a queen can do in the early stage, like with the Scholar's Mate, or in the later stages of the game is imperative to maximizing its potential.

When it comes to trading pieces, you can refer to the table on page 233 to guide you toward the correct decision in most cases. In Part One, it was sufficient for you to say "we each get three points, so it is a fair trade"—not anymore. In intermediate play and beyond, almost every trade that occurs has positives and negatives associated with it, and it is up to you to understand what those are.

The CCA checklist—checks, captures, attacks—is a comprehensive tool to scan for your opponent's ideas, the most forcing moves for yourself, and how to formulate a plan from there. Through many hundreds, if not thousands, of practice games, this checklist will be running in the back of your mind constantly, pushing you to make strong plans and moves.

Use this QR code to review the many concepts we covered in this final chapter.

KEY TERMS AND CONCEPTS

Attack: When a piece is threatening to capture an enemy piece.

Attraction: A tactic in which a piece is sacrificed to lure an opponent's valuable piece (king or queen) into a more vulnerable position.

Backwards Pawn: A pawn that is not necessarily isolated but which cannot move forward without being captured, and which isn't defended by any other pawns.

Battery: Arranging two or more attacking pieces on the same rank, file, or diagonal in order to attack enemy pieces and/or the enemy king.

Blockade: A situation where enemy pieces stand in front of advancing pawns, preventing any forward progress.

Capture: When one piece moves to a square occupied by an enemy piece, thus permanently removing the enemy piece from the game.

Castling: A special move where a king slides 2 squares toward either of the rooks, with the rook hopping over the king and standing adjacent. Only possible when there are no pieces between the king and rook, neither the king nor rook have moved previously, not currently in check, and none of the squares the king is sliding through are attacked by an enemy piece.

Check: An attack on a king by an enemy piece.

Checkmate: An attack on a king from which the king cannot escape, meaning victory for the attacking player.

Closed Position: A position in which very few pawns have been traded and there are few open files and diagonals.

Counterplay: When a player under attack finds a way to attack or pose their own threats.

Danger Levels: Responding to a threat on a piece with a move that threatens an opposing piece of equal or greater value.

Defend: When a piece is positioned so that it can capture back an enemy piece if the aggressor were to capture a friendly piece first.

Deflection: A tactic in which you sacrifice a piece to draw away an enemy piece that is otherwise preventing the loss of material and/or checkmate.

Development: Moving your pieces (bishops, knights, rooks, and queen) from their starting positions to more active squares.

Discovered Attack: A tactic in which a player moves one piece to reveal another piece behind it that is creating a threat. Often, both pieces create separate threats.

Discovered Check: A tactic in which a player moves one piece to reveal another attacking piece behind it that checks the enemy king.

Elo: A numerical rating that quantifies a chess player's skill level relative to other players.

Endgame: The final phase of the game, loosely defined as when more than half the pieces and pawns have been traded.

En Passant: A special move in chess in which, under specific circumstances, a pawn can capture another pawn that has just advanced two squares, despite the pawns being adjacent rather than diagonal.

Exchange Up/Down: When a player has traded a knight or bishop for an opposing rook, they are an "exchange up" or "up an exchange"; conversely, if a player has lost a rook for an opposing knight/bishop, they are "down an exchange."

Fianchetto: The positioning of the bishops one rank up from their starting position so they see across the long diagonal of the board (for White, putting bishops on b2 and g2; for Black, putting bishops on b7 and g7).

File: The vertical columns of a chessboard.

Forced Checkmate: A sequence of moves that, if all the correct moves are found, results in checkmate no matter what the opponent does in response.

Fork: A tactic in chess in which one piece simultaneously attacks two enemy pieces.

Gambit: An opening play in which a player sacrifices material, usually a pawn, in order to gain some other kind of positional or strategic advantage.

Golden Moves: The optimal opening ten moves of any chess game, including taking the center with pawns, developing knights and bishops to active center squares, castling, and connecting the rooks.

Insufficient Checkmating Material: A situation where a player no longer has enough material to ever deliver checkmate.

Isolated Pawn: A pawn standing alone with no pawns of the same color on neighboring files.

Keeping the Tension: A situation where opposing pawns or pieces are able to capture each other but the player or players elect not to trade, usually because it would hand the opponent a tactical or positional initiative.

King Opposition: Positioning a king directly opposite the opposing king with one (or sometimes more) empty squares between them.

Knight Opposition: Positioning a piece relative to a king, if the first piece were a knight, it would be a check. Important concept in checkmating endgames.

Luft: An escape square made for your king after castling by pushing a pawn. Prevents being checkmated on the final rank of the board.

Middlegame: The second phase of the game, between opening and endgame. Begins when previously explored openings reach a new position based on past games.

Opening: The initial phase of the game in which players traditionally fight for the center, develop their pieces, and castle.

Open Position: A position in which many pawns have been traded, so there are lots of empty squares on various files, ranks, and diagonals.

Passed Pawn: A pawn of either color that cannot be stopped from reaching the far side of the board by any opposing pawns.

Pawn Chain: A diagonal line of pawns of the same color, each protected by the pawn behind it.

Pawn Structure: How the pawns of each side are placed in any given position.

Perpetual Check: A tactic in which a player is able to deliver an endless sequence of checks on the enemy king, resulting in a draw.

Pin (Absolute): A tactic in chess in which a piece is unable to move because doing so would expose an attack on the king (which is illegal).

Pin (Relative): A tactic in chess in which a piece is unable to move because doing so would expose a higher-value piece to being captured.

Promotion: A special rule in chess where a pawn becomes either a bishop, knight, rook, or queen (the player's choice) upon reaching the far side of the board.

Rank: The horizontal rows of a chessboard. Numbered 1–8.

Removing the Defender: A tactic in which a player attacks a piece defending another piece or preventing checkmate, resulting in the winning of material.

Resignation: When a player concedes the match, usually because they are certain to eventually lose.

Rook Lift: A plan in chess to bring a rook forward and across, to ultimately threaten enemy pieces or certain weak squares.

Sacrifice: When a player gives up a piece for a piece of lesser value in order to make a bigger gain in subsequent moves, either by winning more material or checkmating the enemy king.

Skewer: A tactic in chess in which a player attacks a high-value piece that, when the high-value piece moves out of danger, reveals another piece behind that can subsequently be captured.

Space: Squares controlled in the opponent's territory, that is, their half of the board.

Stalemate: A situation where a king is not in check but where the player has no legal moves, meaning the game ends in a draw.

Strategy: Long-term plans in chess to gain and maintain positional advantage.

Tactics: Combinations of moves that result in a checkmate, winning of material, or positional advantage.

Tempo: When moves are made that gain initiative and force the opponent into a defensive response.

Trade: When one piece captures an enemy piece and the opponent is able to capture back with a different piece. Often, trades are of equal value.

Variation: A subset of moves that emerge from a particular opening.

Weakness: A piece or square in a player's position that is not defended or is insufficiently defended.

Zugzwang: A situation in chess where a player has to move but any move they make will worsen their position.

Zwischenzug: The insertion of an "in between" move, usually very forcing, before playing the expected or obvious move afterward.

ACKNOWLEDGMENTS

First, I want to give a warm thanks to everyone who made this book possible. Jordan Lees not only suggested that I should write a book, but also helped me every step of the way. My agent, Luba Ostashevsky, taught me everything about the book industry and managed so many fine details of the process—without her, this project may not have reached the finish line. My wonderful editor, Kaitlin Ketchum, along with everyone at Ten Speed, worked tirelessly to brainstorm, conceptualize, and implement so much of the text and visuals—for them I am also tremendously grateful.

When I was six years old, my parents were trying to decide what after-school classes I should take. My mom advocated for chess, since it was part of our Russian-Jewish background, and all our relatives knew how to play. My dad, however, thought art class was better. He figured I liked to mess around with paint, and I was too hyper for something like chess.

Seeing as though you are reading this book and not looking at one of my paintings in a museum, I think my mom made the right decision. Thank you, Mom.

My dad—despite his initial suspicions—became my childhood sparring partner and traveled with me to nearly all my classes and tournaments. I would have never fallen in love with chess if it had not been for his efforts. Thank you, Dad.

My parents split up when I was very young, so my grandparents were also heavily involved in my life and were my emotional support system. Having three homes may sound like a lavish lifestyle, but not when you commute back and forth with your belongings in a backpack as a young kid. Without my grandparents, I would have never known stability. Thank you both.

As we fast-forward to this part of my career, I want to thank the chess fans who have been immensely supportive of my work. This book would not be possible without you.

And lastly, there is Lucy. You captivate me, inspire me, and push me to be the best version of myself every single day. Words cannot describe how much you mean to me. I love you.

ABOUT THE AUTHOR

Levy Rozman, known online as GothamChess, is an International Master and former professional chess instructor from New York. In the early stage of his career, Levy taught chess to hundreds of students and led a scholastic chess program to multiple city and state championships. Since 2020, he has shifted his focus to creating chess content online, and now runs the largest chess YouTube channel. Known for his educational clips and recaps of major tournaments, Levy has quickly become a staple for players of all levels to join the chess community and learn more about the royal game. You can find Levy on YouTube at www.youtube.com/gothamchess.

INDEX

Published in the United States by Ten Speed Press, an imprint of
Random House, a division of the Crown Publishing Group, New York.
TenSpeed.com

Ten Speed Press and the Ten Speed Press colophon are registered
trademarks of Penguin Random House LLC.

Illustrations on cover and page i by KurArt, pages ii and vi by Максим
Лебедик, and pages x, 14, and 120 by Olga; courtesy of Adobestock.

Typefaces: Doni Sukma's Bauziet, Malou Verlomme's Madera,
and TypeType Team's TTFors

Library of Congress Cataloging-in-Publication Data is on file with
the publisher.

Hardcover ISBN: 978-1-9848-6207-5
eBook ISBN: 978-1-9848-6208-2

Printed in China

Editor: Kaitlin Ketchum | Production editor: Serena Wang
Editorial assistant: Kausaur Fahimuddin
Designer: Emma Campion
Production designer: Mari Gill
Production manager: Dan Myers
Copyeditor: Tom Pitoniak | Proofreader: Rita Madrigal
Indexer: Jay Kreider
Publicist: Kristin Casemore | Marketer: Brianne Sperber

10 9 8 7 6 5 4 3 2

First Edition